Glorious
INDOOR
gardens

MICHELE DRISCOLL ALIOTO

photographs by JOHN M. HALL

Stewart, Tabori & Chang • New York

Glorious
INDOOR
gardens

Published in 2002 by
Stewart, Tabori & Chang
A Company of La Martinière Groupe
115 West 18th Street
New York, NY 10011

Export Sales to all countries except Canada, France,
and French-speaking Switzerland:
Thames and Hudson Ltd.
181A High Holborn
London WC1V 7QX England

Canadian Distribution:
Canadian Manda Group
One Atlantic Avenue, Suite 105
Toronto, Ontario M6K 3E7 Canada

Library of Congress Cataloging-in-Publication Data
Alioto, Michelle Driscoll.
  Glorious indoor gardens / by Michelle Driscoll Alioto ; photographs by
John M. Hall.
     p. cm.
  ISBN 1-58479-193-4
  1. Indoor gardens—United States. 2. Indoor gardening—United
States. I. Hall, John M. II. Title.
  SB419 .A43 2002
  635.9'65--dc21
                            2001054934

EDITED BY Marisa Bulzone and Elaine Schiebel
DESIGNED BY Nina Barnett
GRAPHIC PRODUCTION BY Kim Tyner

The text of this book was composed in Adobe Garamond
Printed in CS Graphics PTE, Ltd. in Singapore

10 9 8 7 6 5 4 3 2 1

First Printing

To my dear husband Joe

and to our sweet
Magdalena and Nicholas,
whose gestation and birth paralleled this book
and who inspired me with anticipation and joy every step of the way

Contents

INTRODUCTION

Chapter One

SUBURBAN SUNROOMS

Wilmette Farmhouse Patina 17
The Garden's a Stage:
  Accessorizing the Indoor Garden 22
Lake Forest Painter's Paradise 25
Plants: Green Clean Machines 31

Chapter Two

A GARDEN WITHIN A GARDEN

Palm Beach Grand Loggia 36
Container Gardening 44
Southampton Pool House
  Hospitality 47
How Does Your Child's Garden Grow? 52

Chapter Three

**RARE AND DELIGHTFUL
HOME COLLECTIONS**

Scottsdale Magical Desert 59
Growing Succulents Indoors 66
Houston Fish Tale 69
Hydroponics: Gardening without Soil 74
Palm Beach Orchidaceous 76
Growing Orchids Indoors 82

Chapter Four

CITY LIVING AND AGRARIAN COMFORT

New York Soaring Green Vistas 88
Making Terrariums and Wardian Cases 94
Georgetown Historic Greenhouse 97
Growing Ferns Indoors 104

Chapter Five

GRAND AND FORMAL:
PRIVATE CONSERVATORIES

Greenwich Indoor Retreat 111
Building a Garden under Glass 118
Montgomery Palm Court 120
Designing with Plants 126

Chapter Six

LIVING WITH PROFUSION

Soho Urban Jungle 132
Creating Light Where It Isn't 138
San Francisco Jewel Box 140

Appendix A

CARING FOR
YOUR INDOOR PLANTS 148

Light
Temperature
Humidity
Watering
Pests and Diseases
Fertilizing
Growing Bulbs Indoors

Appendix B

PLANT LISTS 152

Bulbs for Indoors
Ferns for Indoors
Orchids for Indoors
Palms for Indoors
Plants for Children
Plants for Terrariums
Plants That Clean the Air
Plants for Beginning Hydroculture
Succulents for Indoors

Appendix C

RESOURCES 157

Acknowledgments

INTRODUCTION

INDOOR GARDENING SATISFIES OUR YEARNING FOR NATURE, reminds us of the symbiotic relationship we have with plants, and takes us back to our roots. It allows us to ignore the inevitability of the seasons and enjoy a verdant summer day, even as the wet wind howls outside the door.

This passion to be closer to nature year-round is evident in the creative, often eccentric tribulations that plant lovers have been willing to endure to grow plants indoors. They've sailed across perilous oceans, lived through harrowing adventures, and squandered family fortunes to bring home exotic plant specimens that can only survive indoors, and then they built mammoth glass monuments to house them.

For centuries gardeners have endeavored to lift the winter blues by bringing the wonder of nature into their living rooms. They've learned to extend the growing season, replicate the tropics, prolong the harvest, and use their creative resources to design with plant life, transporting the magical, healing spirit of the outdoors into their private living spaces. The ancient Greeks devised ingenious methods to grow plants indoors under artificial conditions, and the Romans built the first greenhouses, made of thin partitions of transparent mica rock.

Umbrellas offer a retreat from the hot afternoon sun, as well
as setting the comfortable mood in this elegant sunroom.

But not until much later in history did indoor gardening, as we know it today, come into existence. The modern-day passion for indoor gardening was heralded by the arrival in Europe between the seventeenth and nineteenth centuries of shiploads of rare, bizarre, and never-seen-before plants from exotic destinations all over the world. Orchids, camellias, palms, cacti, bromeliads, and ferns arrived at port from China, North and South America, Africa, the Philippines, and Madagascar, to the astonishment of plant lovers. The craze these treasures inspired would revolutionize gardening, create new industries, impact the economy, develop a new art form, make sane people frantic, and sweep throughout Europe and the Americas like a wildfire. The rarest plants could drive men to homicide, and a single prized specimen could fetch the price of a fine town house.

From the early 1700s, glasshouses were being built and filled with lush international assortments of tender tropical plants. The conservatory became popular with the aristocracy and the wealthy, as a place to enjoy the pleasures of the outdoors while being sheltered from the elements, and as a natural transition between the house and the garden.

Ornately decorated orangeries, their brightly lit interiors extravagantly furnished with fine carvings and statuary, became *de rigueur* for grand homes. Here hundreds of orange trees, camellias, orchids, palms, and other exotic plants were coddled during the winter; in the summer the plants were moved into the garden, and the orangery became a ballroom for summer entertaining. Queen Anne referred to hers as a "summer supper room."

Not until the late 1800s, with the discovery of methods to manufacture glass inexpensively, would middle-class enthusiasts be able to enjoy the hobby as well. Modest conservatories were built onto small family homes, providing extra light and warmth as well as an ideal space for growing exotic warm-climate plants.

Conservatories and greenhouses are still popular, but gardeners today know that many tropical, Mediterranean, and desert plants can do just as well in the conditions of our own homes, given the proper care. Although a conservatory or greenhouse is an ideal environment, a kitchen windowsill, a steamy bathroom, a well-lighted dining room, or a basement family room with supplemental lighting can provide all a healthy plant needs.

Indoor plants are delightful decorative accessories; these "living furnishings" can beautify and give life to a decor like few other things, while caring for them promotes tranquillity and offers a magical retreat.

It is my hope that the gardeners and indoor gardens in this book will inspire you to take a small vignette from an extravagant setting and find a place for it in your own environment, or to develop a grand idea from a modest setting for your personal castle.

Above all, I hope you are blessed with the ability to cultivate peaceful beauty and nature right in your home that celebrates your unique style and flair.

Plants with varying leaf shapes, textures, and shades of green can be grouped to make a harmonious setting.

CHAPTER

ONE

·❦·

*Suburban
Sunrooms*

A sunroom suggests ease; a welcoming place from another era, filled with the fragrance of moist earth, with planted window boxes and hanging ferns. One thinks of well-used faded chintz cushions, rattan furniture, and always an ottoman; easy reading magazines and summer novels, and the warm sun on your shoulder. It's an informal, lazy room that soothes the soul and inspires the gardener in all of us.

A sunroom doesn't necessarily have a glass ceiling, although some do. It can double as a breakfast room, a sitting room adjacent to the bedroom or an addition to the kitchen. When I was growing up, many of the homes in our neighborhood had small sunrooms with large wood-framed windows, which were sometimes used as bedrooms if the need arose. Lots of light, large windows, and an airy, sunny exposure are the only requisites.

The best sunrooms offer a view of the garden and bridge the inside and the out. Like porches, they are popular in many country architectures because they help to transport the inhabitants into nature without exposing them to the elements. A sunroom can be one of the most comfortable and delightful rooms in the house, and one that is sure to draw in the family and their guests all year long.

Previous spread: A lovely collection of antique garden furniture and accessories greatly enhances the old-world mood of this century-old greenhouse.

Far left: A bookshelf finds new life as a creative way to display plants.

Left: A terrarium set against the natural backdrop of the garden outside also benefits from the window's indirect light.

Facing page: Old-fashioned charm is married to contemporary comfort in this lush sunroom.

WILMETTE FARMHOUSE PATINA

BUILT A CENTURY AGO BY AN APPLE FARMER and nurseryman, these charming cottagelike structures have come full circle since their construction. Originally an old farmhouse and farm implement store, they once stood on a rural midwestern road. Today this has grown into a busy suburban boulevard, and the buildings are the home and offices of modern-day nursery owners and award-winning garden designers Craig Bergmann and James Grigsby.

An antique greenhouse, the only part of the present-day home that was not on the original plan, has an equally romantic history. Built in the early 1900s for the Winnetka High School by Lord and Burnham Conservatories, it was languishing in a heap of glass and cast iron when it was discovered in 1965 by the athletic director of the high school, a former owner of the house. He purchased it for $1, brought it home, and—without the benefit of a plan or instructions—rebuilt it over the back porch of the old farmhouse.

Facing page: Trompe l'oeil vines wind around faux marble supporting posts, underscoring the richness of the antiques and collection of plants.

Right: James and Craig enjoy caring for their greenhouse plants together.

Above: The entrance to the greenhouse from the garden, flanked by clipped evergreens, builds up a delightful anticipation in the visitor.

Below: Topiary forms outside the greenhouse set a mood with texture, color, and a playful mixture of formal and organic shapes.

When Grigsby first saw the house—one of the oldest homes in Wilmette, Illinois—he was immediately captivated. It became available for sale several years later, and in the early 1980s, Grigsby and Bergmann eagerly snapped it up. "We were committed to staying here a long time, and we knew we could make this home and garden reflect the things we loved," says Bergmann.

Although the greenhouse had a rusting frame, and the original roof was in desperate disrepair, they still felt it had great promise—"It was certainly dilapidated, but it had great charm and was architecturally a wonderful structure." The greenhouse was also a boon to Bergmann and Grigsby, who had recently founded a new landscaping business. Although it was necessary to replace all the glass, install heaters and fans, and build benches for plants, the renovated space was vital for raising starter plants, seedlings, and cuttings.

Self-proclaimed "evangelists of midwestern gardening," with a specialty in English garden style and a penchant for unusual plants and cuttings from Europe, the two set out in their new business to redefine the possibilities of gardening in the heart of the country. "Gardening here in the Midwest was always about sustenance. It was about growing nothing more than tomatoes and corn, and we wanted people to understand that it is possible to have great gardens here," says James.

Over the years, the business grew; with its move to a twenty-acre European-style nursery in Winthrop Harbor with five exterior gardens and twenty-three greenhouses, the comparatively inefficient antique greenhouse became redundant. It was at that time that they decided to convert it into a private conservatory to house their personal collection of plants, antiques, garden furniture, and accessories.

Today the glasshouse in the old farmhouse has become the focus of Bergmann and Grigsby's home and garden, a delightfully fragrant and verdant trove of unique plants and unusual collectibles, with an aged patina reminiscent of earlier years.

Lush hanging ferns and a giant kentia palm help to create a mood suggestive of a century-old conservatory. "The giant potted palms have a period feel to them, like the ones you might see in the grand old hotels with the large, long fronds. Ours has really gotten too big for the room, but we don't have the heart to get rid of it. It's a member of the family now, so we just duck," says Craig, laughing.

With their talent for English garden style and a penchant for unusual plants and cuttings from Europe, the greenhouse was essential.

Above, left to right: Echeveria *rosettes, elegant in their simplicity, are easy to care for; antique containers and ornaments; perennials in pots, like this dianthus, can be changed seasonally to keep the look fresh.*

Bergmann and Grigsby like to collect unusual plants. "We have some odd-looking ferns that we like to grow and some epiphytic things like orchids and cacti, which can withstand the rigors of our busy life but also have interesting foliage or an interesting architectural aspect," says Craig.

Maidenhair ferns flutter in the soft breeze, and rabbit-foot ferns with furlike extended rhizomes in old textured concrete planters exemplify the unique look favored by the proprietors. "It looks like the stump has sprouted branches because it is the same color as the mossy-colored concrete pot. We love that kind of thing," says Craig.

Light-loving orchids (*Vanda* sp.) with showy blossoms hang from the ceiling, and *Paphiopedilum* sp. orchids that crave the ambient light and cool humidity of the conservatory are nestled down lower. *Odontoglossums* resembling crawling spiders, and unusually vibrant bicolored and orange cattleyas, help to complete an impressive orchid collection.

A romantic fifteen-year-old night-blooming cereus in an antique rusticated urn blooms several times a year with six to eight ten-inch blossoms at a time. "It's a wonderful fragrance, and when you walk into the conservatory it makes you think Ava Gardner's been invited to dinner," James jokes.

The bold foliage of a thirty-year-old clivia that measures four feet across, given to them ten years ago, blooms in the spring with dramatic orange-and-yellow blossoms, followed by bright red summer fruits. "The color is common, but the blossom, size, and health of this plant are amazing," says Craig.

The patterned leaves of rex begonias help to enrich the verdant surroundings. They are a favorite plant of Craig's: "I have a real thing for rex begonias because of the beautiful and interesting leaves. To me they are spectacular."

The partners, who have two Tibetan terriers appropriately named Forest and Rosy, also share a love of art. James is a graduate of the Institute of Design at the Illinois Institute of Technology and a former art professor at the Art Institute of Chicago. His expertise is evident in the pair's extensive collection of American and European antiques and American folk art.

The owners' interests and flair are apparent in the furnishings and accessories in the conservatory. Dark green cast-iron furniture made by Kramer Brothers in 1880 creates a comfortable seating area for enjoying the surroundings. Nineteenth- and early-twentieth-century pots from France, Belgium, and England serve as containers for an assortment of plants. A favorite is a rare but fragile forty-inch-tall clay strawberry pot from France they found in a local antique store. Old watering cans from England and a delightful assortment of more than thirty birdhouses from all over the United States, which line the rafters and windowsills, add to the ambience of this lovely room. An old grate serves as a screen door to the entry, and an ornamental handle, stumbled across at a flea market, is welded on to complete the look.

To enhance the patina of the room and add to the aged look of the walls, an artist was hired to paint a mural on the south wall of an American landscape in autumn. Steps made of porous stone and a floor of patterned bluestone and brick encourage, to the owners' delight, the natural growth of algae and mosses.

Craig, who has a degree in biology and botany from DePaul University, received his state license as a landscape architect by virtue of his eighteen years of experience and expertise. He has had a deep connection to nature and plants since his Illinois childhood. His father gave him his own garden next to the garage when he was five years old, encouraging this passion. "It was a very nurturing childhood and one that really fits into my love of plants," says Craig. He remembers fondly the woods across from his childhood home, with special yellow violets that he wanted to transplant to his own garden, and his father's lesson that for every yellow violet he removed, he needed to give back to the woods by transplanting the purple ones from his own garden. "My parents were great at building respect for nature," he says; "it was a wonderful childhood that shaped my life and helps me appreciate this beautiful place."

The conservatory helps to alleviate the stress of a long workday, Craig explains: "When we are in the greenhouses at the nursery with so much to do, we are always thinking about what is not done, what needs to be done, what is not doing well, but here it is different. When something doesn't make it, if the wind or the dog knocks something over it isn't so bothersome anymore. We just view it as an opportunity to bring in a new friend to join the family, because these plants are our friends."

The conservatory is a favorite place to entertain, and they often have lunch there or invite friends in for cocktails before dinner. "Friends come in to this room with the giant saucer magnolia overhanging outside the greenhouse, and on a spring night we look up and see the flowers on the magnolias through the glass, and it is pretty transporting," says James. But it also welcomes solitude. "I'll go shovel snow and ice, and then I'll sit down in front of the heater with the dogs to warm up, and it's kind of fun to feel that one minute you are knocking off all this snow, and the next minute you are sitting in this tropical spot in the middle of Illinois," says Craig. "We always say it is a little piece of the Yucatán in the wintertime."

The owners' collection of antique birdhouses from all over America share the room with an uncommon brassia *hybrid. A* Pathiopedilum naudiae *is displayed on a pedestal.*

Accessorizing the Indoor Garden

FROM THE WHIMSY OF A TINY KITCHEN WINDOW BOX to the formal elegance of a classical fountain, indoor garden accessories underscore design and structure and express individuality. Ornamentation can help to set a mood, accentuate beauty, and be utilitarian too.

Weathered wheelbarrows, stone pots, a child's wagon, or an old tin washtub, colorfully stocked with perennials or annuals, are eye-catchers in any garden room. Place them at the entry, or with a seating arrangement. Be creative. Some of the most unique and effective containers are right in your own backyard, garage, or attic, waiting to be discovered.

Create an ambience that will suggest a natural environment. A small freestanding fountain in the center of the room, for instance, will immediately attract the eye and be an important centerpiece. Used inconspicuously in a corner or against a wall, it will bring a charming element of surprise. Fountains and indoor ponds add peace and natural music to a setting and raise the spirits. Fish or birds can create an authentic, outdoorsy feeling.

Some ornamentation can invoke a smile or be the seed of humor. It is the small details that really count and set the stage for putting your signature on your garden room. A small piece of statuary sitting inconspicuously with a few plants on a kitchen windowsill, a hand-painted birdhouse perched at the foot of a ficus, a collection of seashells used as mulch for your palm—all give personality to a garden. Folk art of all kinds, from homemade bird feeders to colored ceramic bowls or painted cans designed by children, can be creative and effective.

Far left: A bright spray of oncidium *orchids glows against a backdrop of stone artifacts.*

Left: Whimsical painted tin roses sprout from a salvaged architectural detail.

Facing page: Paphiopedilum orchids appreciate the lower light conditions closer to the floor. Rusticated pots and plant stands, an antique terrarium, and stone ornaments and furnishings give a weathered patina to the room.

Furnishings in the garden room invite one to be comfortable, to have a meal, a drink, or to relax and absorb the surroundings. A hand-carved wooden porch swing speaks of the long, lazy days of summer. A weathered Adirondack chair, placed among potted grasses, brings back fond memories of a childhood on the beach. Antiques are better protected indoors and can be effective adornments. Both practical and decorative, garden furnishings set a mood and fulfill a need.

Well-placed objects can fool us by visually enlarging the space, creating intimacy or a new perspective. They delight the eye, invite the body to linger, and highlight the ambience with beauty, history, and even humor. Building a small, elongated pool in the foreground of a garden room gives an illusion of space that will make you think rural. The mirror image created by reflecting water changes the perspective and makes even a tiny space feel larger.

One garden I know has a big-finned 1954 Cadillac, submerged upright in the garden with chrome grille and head-light eyes smiling toward the sun. Although this might not be your idea of agrarian beauty, and it would probably never fit in your living room, it does express exemplary courage. It also serves as a reminder that gardening is an art, after all. And the ornamentation in our indoor garden completes the canvas that only begins with our plantings.

LAKE FOREST PAINTER'S PARADISE

IT TOOK THE IMAGINATIVE EYE OF AN ARTIST to see that in the midst of one of the harshest and most gloomy Illinois winters, light and inspiration could be found in a glasshouse oasis filled with fruit-bearing trees and vibrantly blooming orchids.

When the winter snows arrived in November 2000, thirty-two-year-old landscape artist Yaz Krehbiel, banned by a safety-conscious landlord from his improvised studio on the roof of a Chicago apartment building, knew that work on his eleven-foot cityscape painting would have to be deferred.

In search of a new setting, he took to the suburbs and his parent's nine-and-a-half-acre estate in Lake Forest, Illinois. "There was snow everywhere, and it was really dreary outside, but I walked into the greenhouse, and I was immediately struck by the energy in that room," he says. "There were so many forms and colors, and it was a real refuge from the winter here. I immediately knew the search for new painting possibilities had just ended." Canvases, easel, paints, brushes, rags, and palette were hauled into position on the damp, warm tile floor of the greenhouse among the fuchsias, camellias, pentas, salvias, and heliotropes.

Yaz Krehbiel and his Labrador retriever, Bear.

If the greenhouse generated new excitement and promise for Yaz as an artist, it remained as always an established passion for his mother, Posy Krehbiel, who is a devoted and talented gardener.

Her infatuation began in 1967 when she and her husband John purchased their first home, a renovated barn on three-and-a-half acres. "I didn't know anything about gardening when we bought that property. I was busy with three little children and I was an avid tennis player. My friends didn't have an interest in gardening either," she remembers. "But the property had a wonderful terrace and a very pretty rose garden and a great big empty meadow out in front. I just started picking away at it every year." As the garden developed, so did the enthusiasm, and when they sold the property in 1988, the new occupants became owners of a garden treasure that reflected Posy Krehbiel's twenty-one years of devotion.

That same year the Krehbiels bought a larger home on four-and-a-half acres in Lake Forest. Part of a twelve-acre estate that had been subdivided, the grand redbrick Georgian home was built in 1904 by Benjamin Marshall. The Krehbiels became the eighth owners and were delighted with the attentive care the house had been given over the years. "She was a lucky old girl, this house," says Posy; "she was well cared for."

The garden however, was not as fortunate. Although it had been well maintained over the years, the subdivision into four parcels had erased most of the outline of the original site, and the great artistry of the early design was lost.

Still, Posy was captivated by the promise she saw. Designed in the 1920s by renowned Boston landscape architect Rose Standish Nichols, the garden was considered such a stunning success at the time that the Garden Club of America documented it on slides and donated them to the Smithsonian Institution. "This garden still had wonderful mature trees and hedges and a rose arbor, and in the back of my mind I kept thinking about the way it had been. It was just so appealing that I couldn't wait to begin with it.

From left to right: The working greenhouse, viewed from the garden; rows of plants are nurtured inside,
to be moved into the house or the garden at their peak; blooming orchids, perennials, and bromeliads on a stepladder
bring height and color to a corner of the conservatory.

I was planting before the former owners moved out," Posy admits, laughing.

In 1996 two adjacent homes, part of the original property, became available for sale, and Posy's dream of reconstructing the old garden became a reality. The Krehbiels purchased the lots, and their property grew to include nine-and-one-half acres of the original twelve. The two homes were razed, and they immediately began preparations to return the gardens to their former glory.

The traditional English-style garden was restored to a parklike setting complete with rolling lawns, hundreds of roses, a linden allée, pergolas, white gardens, and countless perennials in muted colors. Grand, mature trees were craned onto the property, and experts from all over the world were brought in to consult. Architects Tom and Kirsten Beeby from Chicago and landscape architect Deborah Nevins from New York worked on the garden concept. Posy consulted with Cliff Miller, a naturalist, and Craig Bergmann, a local landscape architect (see "Wilmette Farmhouse Patina," page 17). Renowned English garden designer and writer Rosemary Verey spent the day reshaping flowerbeds and consulting on perennial color. Penelope Hobhouse, England's grand dame of horticulture, and garden writer Christopher Lloyd came to see and marvel.

Visit the Krehbiels on any day, and you'll find Posy, knees in soil and trowel in hand, working and laughing alongside her gardeners. Her head gardener is horticulturist Marya Padour, who has worked for the family for eight years. "Posy gets very excited about gardening and makes everyone else so happy about it," says Marya. "She's an artist and was born with an eye for putting things together and creating beautiful things. She's also very peppy and a lot of fun to work for. I always joke that if she could sell her energy, she'd have a very profitable business."

As the garden grew, so did the need for greenhouses. "If you are going to garden in Chicago and you want to save any plants," Posy says, "you must have a greenhouse." It was decided that two greenhouses would be necessary. One would be a smaller, working greenhouse in the garden to be used for propagating cuttings and seeds. The other would be attached to the home, and its main function would be to accommodate the growing number of mature plants that Posy had collected or imported from Florida. It would also serve as a comfortable room for the family to gather and a retreat from the trials of winter.

"I'd been investigating this for a long time," says Posy.

Above: The conservatory serves as a bridge between house and garden.

Below: With its elegant restraint, the English-style conservatory complements the the Georgian architecture of the house.

"I went to the Chelsea Garden Show in England to look, and I think I interviewed every single representative in Chicago. The problem was that many companies build glass family rooms, but I wanted a real greenhouse where plants would thrive." For the addition to the home they had an English-style wood-and-glass structure designed, and construction began in 1995. It was fitted with special vents and fans for controlling air circulation, and radiant heat for proper plant maintenance. French terra-cotta floors with drains allow for the plants to be hosed down when necessary, and present an informal and relaxed indoor decor.

Each season transforms the greenhouse. "This room really has two roles for our family," says Yaz. "In the summer it is a lived-in room and becomes an extension of the garden. In the winter it is more of a pure greenhouse overflowing with plants, but still with space for us to go there for dinner or to have tea, or in my case, to paint."

When the winter chill arrives, the lush assortment of lady's slippers and *vanda* orchids, abutilons, cestrums, and pomegranates begin to fill the room with the fragrance of steamy, earthy moisture. Green metal furniture is moved in for dining; on one table a specially designed grid top replaces the glass tabletop, allowing it to serve as a plant stand for some of the dozens of plants brought in from the garden for the winter.

The feeling is one of a dense and moist, yet intimate tropical jungle. Snow gathers on the roof, enclosing the space like a cozy, jungle cocoon. "One of the great moments of the conservatory is the snow on the roof," says Posy. "It is just so beautiful, and it changes everything. You'll be in this room filled with beautiful plants and a white ceiling and very little light, and then the sun comes out and the snow slowly starts rolling off the roof and you go from this sort of a cavelike, intimate feeling to a bright, sunlit day."

The first warm days of the season are reminders to prepare the greenhouse for the next phase. Plans for festive summer lunches are made, canvas umbrellas and summer furniture are brought out of storage, and windows and doors are opened to catch the warm breezes. Cold-sensitive plants that have been housed in the greenhouse all winter are prepared to be returned to their seasonal homes outside in the garden. Shade-loving ferns and lushly blooming tuberous begonias, fancy zonal pelargoniums, and agapanthus with giant purple blooms fill the plant stands, and the room is transformed into a sunny summer porch, center stage to the exterior gardens.

Furnishings and fabrics are changed seasonally and yearly. This year natural wicker sofas are covered in Spanish Iciar de la Concha fabric in a khaki-and-red Aranjuez pattern depicting green gardens and fountains. Some years Posy chooses twig, wicker, or iron furniture, often covered in various Iciar de la Concha fabrics with garden motifs. Four natural canvas market umbrellas create an inviting outdoor feel in the room, and protect it from the summer sun, which becomes intensified by the glass ceiling.

Posy is known for her good humor as well as her kindness, and the garden and greenhouse are open frequently for charitable events and garden club tours. "We open the garden to just about anyone who is breathing," she jokes, minimizing her generosity. The greenhouse is also where the family gathers for Christmas dinners, wedding banquets, winter dining, and summertime iced tea. It's a place that brings garden solace to the winter-weary. "Plants are my friends," says Posy. "And gardening is a passion that gives me true pleasure. It's something I can think about all the time, like having a favorite vacation spot, and even though I may not actually be there, it's always in my head. Having this room allows me to live and be around plants anytime I want and during all the seasons. It's spring fever, it's baseball, it's renewal."

Yaz has found in the greenhouse more than a temporary studio for his latest painting. "I was drawn to paint inside the greenhouse for the same reason I am drawn to it as a person. It is a quiet, very beautiful place and has a reflective, contemplative feeling about it. Going into the greenhouse is like going on a retreat."

The room is transformed to a sunny, summer porch
that is center stage to the exterior gardens.

Green Clean Machines

IF SOMEONE TRIED TO SELL YOU a little green cleaning machine that would clean your house, remove all the toxins, freshen the air, beautify your home, lift your spirits, and cost just a few dollars, you'd be pretty skeptical. But investigate a little deeper, and you'd discover that's exactly how NASA cleans house.

In the 1970s NASA was experimenting with growing crops in sealed chambers to freshen the air and grow food for the space program. They discovered, to their astonishment, that the plants also removed the toxins and poisons in the area. This revelation gave one of their researchers, Dr. Bill Wolverton, an idea: houseplants could serve as little green cleaning machines in our homes. He was aware that formaldehyde and other poisons found in paint, cleaning products, and even carpets, fabrics, and furniture made with chemical dyes and adhesives, as well as many ordinary household products like facial tissues and garbage bags, are toxic traps in our homes that often cause allergies and illness.

Dr. Wolverton left NASA and began researching the effect of houseplants on toxins. He found they were remarkably effective at removing not only poisonous fumes but also the thousands of airborne bacteria and fungi that thrive in our homes. In fact, homes with plant-filled rooms contain 50 to 60 percent fewer airborne molds and bacteria than rooms without plants.

Houseplants, it seems, are happy to allow their leaves to absorb toxic gases and convert them to food, preventing us from inhaling or absorbing them first. Having evolved over millions of years in the rain forest where they had to battle off molds, mildew, and other infectious things, it makes sense they would perform the same way in our homes.

Houseplants not only keep the air clean but also delight our senses with their beauty, and improve the environment by humidifying the air. People who surround themselves with plants, studies show, show lower stress levels. A list of air-cleaning plants is included in the Appendix.

This extravagant bounty of plants delights the eye, while scenting and purifying the air.

CHAPTER

TWO

❦

A Garden
within a
Garden

*G*azebos, pool houses, porches, potting sheds, and loggias all mark transitions in the garden, places where the inside and out meld to create a wonderful new ambience. Making the most of these garden bridges can transform your garden.

The delightful thing about open structures in the garden is that they are entirely exposed, making them integral parts of the landscaping and design, life-size accessories as well as living spaces. Creatively designed, they flatter the landscape, add to the garden's charm, and offer reprieve from the afternoon sun.

Garden shelters can range from a formal loggia for entertaining, to a gazebo that creates a focal point while supporting climbing vines or hanging plants, to a rustic shed for storing garden equipment. They add a vertical element to the garden, especially in spots where trees don't offer height, and provide a quiet spot to watch squirrels and birds and make an intimate connection with nature.

Take advantage of the shelter, shed, or pergola in your garden; imagine it as a secret garden, a private place to relax, or a spot for a romantic rendezvous.

Previous spread: This Palm Beach loggia offers the best of two worlds: expansive views of a magnificent garden and patio, and a sheltering roof.

Facing page: A South Hampton pool house invites the outdoors in while offering protection from the elements.

Right: Sculptural cranes gaze into the formal loggia of this Florida villa.

Palm Beach Grand Loggia

Close your eyes when you enter this Palm Beach loggia and be transported to another time. The warm, moonlit evening is perfumed with the fruity fragrance of the tropics, erasing for the moment the solicitude of the war brewing in Europe. Stylishly dressed couples sway on the polished tile floor as the band plays a foxtrot. The hostess is Consuelo Vanderbilt Balsan, and the scene is Casa Alva, the Mediterranean-style villa she built in 1934 upon returning to America from France.

Open your eyes and enter the new millennium and the home of Maura and Bill Benjamin. Time has passed, and the house and gardens have been altered to accommodate modern lifestyles, but the gracious elegance of the former owner is reflected everywhere, diligently preserved by the Benjamins.

Left: Maura Benjamin and her two bichons frises, Consuela and Buttons.

Facing page: Fine interior fabric is used to upholster the loggia's furniture.

Above: *Tropical breezes carry delightful fragrances to the diners at this table; the tablecloth is made of the same fine fabric as the loggia furniture.*

Opposite, from left to right: *Phalaenopsis orchids, heavy with bloom; built-in cabinet and treillage work, installed by former owner Consuelo Vanderbilt Balsan, sets off orchids; hand-turned treillage and a Portuguese tile mural typify the home's fine craftsmanship.*

Below: *Bill Benjamin constructed the Italian carved stone fountain, planted with papyrus, water lilies, water hyacinths, and duckweed.*

Avoiding the city bustle of Palm Beach, Consuelo and her husband, Jacques Balsan, chose 100 acres of wild jungle-like acres in Manatee Cove on Hypoluxo Island in Florida. A well-respected architect of the day, Maurice Fatio, was hired to design the home, which was eventually enlarged to its present size of 24,000 square feet. With gracious arches and columns and a tiled roof, the Mediterranean home was planned around acres of lush tropical gardens and a private nine-hole golf course. Rooms from centuries-old European palaces and villas were shipped to Florida and fitted into the new construction.

The original home also included an exposed-beam loggia that connected the living and dining rooms and opened out on the golf course. Several years after the house was built, Consuelo purchased a whimsical hand-painted Portuguese mural, which inspired her to change her conception of the loggia. The beams were enclosed, artists installed intricate hand-turned treillage, and the loggia became a garden room, with one side left open to the verdant views beyond.

Consuelo and Jacques entertained socialites of the day as well as heads of state, artists, and future history makers. Winston Churchill vacationed there with his family in the springtime, and had a bedroom named for him. He was often seen puffing on his cigar and wandering pensively throughout the gardens, or painting by the swimming pool. It is said that his Iron Curtain speech was written from his room over the kitchen.

The impressive history of this house, however, does not dampen its hominess. "We feel so comfortable here; it is a real home," says Maura, "and we have a sense that we really belong here. Yet I also feel as if we are curators of the house, as if our job here is to preserve this wonderful place."

Another phase of its history was born in 1957 when Bill Benjamin purchased the property. The hundred acres were subdivided, and all but fifteen acres surrounding the home were sold as separate properties. Bill converted the home into a private social club called the Manalapan Club, a popular spot for dining, bridge, golf tournaments, and swimming. In 1975 the club was closed, and the house remained vacant until 1980, when Bill allowed the Junior League to use it for a decorator showcase.

Bill and Maura, married only a year, attended the opening-night cocktail party together. "I was so taken aback when I saw it. I thought, by God, this is the most beautiful home I've ever been in. The decorators used very

The loggia is one of the most beautiful things about the house. It incorporates the inside with the outside and it is a real garden room.

low lights and candles to hide all the flaws because the house had fallen into such disrepair, but I didn't care about any of those things." The third and last stage of the history of Casa Alva began that night. "I knew as soon as I walked in that I had to take it on," said Maura. A few months later the Benjamins moved in.

New air-conditioning and heating were installed, a new roof was added, and electricity and plumbing were overhauled. "It was unbelievable how much had to be done once we got started," Maura remembers. "My friends would come over and see we were living in a war zone. Knowing how I loved to be surrounded by beautiful things they were horrified and would say 'Maura, what are you thinking?' and I'd just say 'Oh come and see my beautiful new roof.' It was a labor of love."

One of her favorite rooms needed the most work. "The loggia is one of the most beautiful things about the house. It incorporates the inside with the outside, and it is a real garden room." One of the first projects was the restoration of the crumbing treillage. "It was almost impossible to find an artist who still did this kind of work," she says. "Finally we found someone, and he worked for weeks. The work was so involved and tedious, and when he left he handed me the tools and brushes and paint and said, 'I don't think I ever want to see this room again,'" she laughs.

Although the loggia is open to the garden on one side, Maura considers it an integral part of the house. "It is important in the layout because it's an extension to the living and dining rooms. I wouldn't think, for instance, of using an outdoor fabric on the furniture. I only use fine

*The one outstanding job of the season is the one he is doing for
Mr. and Mrs. Jacques Balsan. (She was the Duchess of
Marlborough, and Harold Vanderbilt's sister.) They have bought
an island down here, and Maurice is to build them a house,
swimming pool, tennis court, and gardens. Not on an elaborate scale,
but they have such exquisite taste in everything they do.*

—From a letter by Eleanor Fatio, March 19, 1934

*The original loggia (above) was built in the early 1930s,
with the home; several years later Consuelo Vanderbilt Balsan
renovated it, adding the Portuguese tile mural, and removing
the exposed-beam ceiling (facing page). Photo above courtesy
of the Alexandra Fatio collection.*

indoor upholstery fabric because that is the way we live in the room."

The property around the house today covers six acres of landscaped grounds maintained by professionals. "The tropical gardens here are beautiful," says Maura, "and I love orchids, but the truth is I prefer the English style of gardening I do in my summer house in Maine. All the gardening I do in Florida takes place in the loggia, so that makes this room very important to me." The details of the loggia are striking. Many decades of use have buffed red Cuban ceramic tiles to a brilliant shine. The green treillage work, a fine example of a unique and prized art, suggests a

sunny outdoor garden. Glass and iron lanterns originally placed by Consuelo complement iron wall sconces added by the Benjamins. Ceiling fans gently stir the air, refreshing both plants and people.

Against the rich green foliage, white blossoms illuminate the loggia like many little lights. Maura, who is a representative for Christie's fine art auctioneers, has an eye for the smallest details. "I prefer to plant almost everything in white, or very muted pastels, because it is so chic, and visually the white blossoms with yellow walls and dark green shutters are so pleasing when you look out to all the dark green lawn. All-white or light-colored flowers, which are often harder to grow and harder to find, complement the surroundings, whereas bright-colored flowers divert the eye."

Phalaenopsis orchids are among her favorites plants, and the large open-faced blooms are placed carefully around the room on tables. "I adore orchids," says Maura. "They absolutely love it here, and they just keep blooming and blooming. I think it must be just the right amount of gentle breeze, moisture in the air, and light." To satisfy their need for low light, Boston ferns are planted in pots in the back of the room; white impatiens overflow from freestanding pots, and gloxinia and azaleas are planted seasonally.

The adjacent patio, an exterior extension to the loggia, is planted to complement it. White geraniums overflow from terra-cotta pots, and the fragrance of gardenias in giant tubs permeates the air. An exception to Maura's white or pastel blossom rule is a vibrant orange bougainvillea; dominating the threshold between the loggia and outdoor patio, it adds to the Mediterranean flavor of the decor. "I love the bright-colored bougainvillea because its color and size really guides your eye to the outside view, and it looks nice with the color of the house and green shutters."

The Benjamins replaced the original terrazzo patio floor with Florida's native coquina stone. To satisfy his love for the sound of running water, Bill built an Italian carved stone fountain, complete with a stone boy with dolphin, and planted it with aquatics such as papyrus, water lilies, water hyacinths, and duckweed.

The loggia is the site for a yearly Easter brunch, and every three or four weeks one or two dozen friends come to dinner to enjoy the beautiful environment. "We have cocktails or after-dinner coffee in the loggia and dinner in the dining room," says Maura. Guests can gaze out over expansive lawns, Consuelo's former golf course, palm trees, and a full acre of majestic banyans—a breathtaking sight that a friend once described as a "great cathedral of banyans."

"People love to linger in the loggia, it is just so beautiful," Maura says. "I look around in this gorgeous room, or I come out to care for the plants and see out to that beautiful crown of banyans marching down the golf course. I reminisce about what this room has seen, and I can hardly believe the beauty of it all or my own good fortune to be here."

This dramatic photograph, taken in 1932, records the view of Consuelo Vanderbilt Balsan's private golf course (courtesy of Alexandra Fatio Collection). A contemporary image of the same view appears on pages 32–33.

Container Gardening

THE ART OF CONTAINER GARDENING IS NEARLY AS OLD as gardening itself. The gardens of ancient Greece held shrub-filled clay pots, the Romans grew herbs and vegetables in stone troughs, and the Chinese nurtured flowering plants in ornate vases before the Christian era began.

Most indoor gardening is done in pots, and in many ways container gardening has advantages over traditional beds. Pests are easier to control; individual plants can be treated according to their specific needs; trailing plants, often climbers in the garden, can cascade from hanging baskets; pots can be grouped creatively for beautiful displays; and the containers themselves can be a decorative addition to the indoor garden. Look for pots with good drainage that are heavy enough to provide stability, and large enough to allow for root growth and to hold sufficient soil to supply the plant with ample water and nutrients. Plan to repot as the plant grows, but be aware that some orchids and other plants like to be slightly root bound, and others with shallow rooting systems, such as cactus, do well in half pots.

A wide selection of attractive and unusual containers made of wood, ceramic, glass, china, or terra-cotta will accommodate houseplants stylishly. Teapots, watering cans, copper kettles, and even old boots can be creatively used as temporary novelty containers. Single plants can be left in their original containers and placed directly inside an ornamental container or cachepot, which will double as a saucer to protect furnishings and floors if it doesn't have drainage holes. If the height of the container allows, an inch or two of gravel on the bottom of the

Facing page, left: As decorative as they are functional, miniature clay pots, a stone trough, and a metal watering can all make charming plant holders.

Right: This delightful ceramic porcupine, in lieu of quills, has holes in which to arrange flowers.

cachepot, with a bit of fresh water, can increase humidity, a boon to most houseplants. However, take care that plants do not sit in standing water; they should drain completely after watering before being placed back into the decorative container.

Sphagnum moss can be tucked around the base of the plant to make a decorative finish, which also helps prevent soil from drying out. Tuck a few small annuals or blooming perennials into the moss for a temporary touch of color.

If planting directly into a pot, make certain it has proper drainage. If the pot is going to be placed on a floor or table that needs to be protected, place a nonabsorbent saucer underneath. Clay containers tend to sweat, and even though the pot appears to be dry, it can damage furniture.

As clay pots age, they often develop an attractive coating of green moss on the outside. To encourage this, spray the exterior of the pot with a diluted solution of buttermilk and water. New clay pots should be soaked in water for at least an hour before use so they do not draw moisture from the soil. It is important to clean the interior of pots thoroughly before reusing, to prevent the spread of soilborne plant diseases. Use a stiff brush and warm water mixed with a little household bleach and dishwashing liquid, and rinse well.

Line metal containers with plastic to prevent them from leaching minerals into the growing medium. Wooden containers can also be lined in plastic to prevent rotting.

SOUTHAMPTON POOL HOUSE HOSPITALITY

IT WAS JOAN CARL'S PASSION FOR GARDENING AND LOVE OF HISTORY, combined with a fantasy of an eighteenth-century orangery, that inspired the decor of her newly renovated pool house. "I could just see a place in another time where ladies would go to get out of the sun, and still be surrounded by nature in a formal and contained way," she says. Lush Boston ferns cascade from English wire baskets, coral begonias peek out from imported wall planters, and eight-foot palms create an indoor umbrella; the scene is pleasantly reminiscent of another time, yet the setting is in a thoroughly modern American family home.

The idea for the modern-day conservatory, reconstructed on the site of an old bathhouse, was born early on a spring afternoon in 1994. When Joan and Bernard Carl arrived from their Washington, D.C. home to view the Southampton property with a real estate agent, they knew the

Facing page: Wire furniture lends a breezy openness to this pool house, softened by palms, ferns, ivies, and begonias.

Right: Joan Carl and her King Charles spaniel Lillibet get away to the pool house for an afternoon of reading and relaxing.

Above: The pool house, seen across a rolling lawn and a vibrant perennial border.

Below: This charming nineteenth-century fountain, with a lead figure personifying Abundance, was purchased in England.

classic white-shingled Hampton home would need some renovation. Diverting attention from the repairs the house needed, the agent focused on the mesmerizing sound and intoxicating fragrance of the ocean breezes, the grand old willow and linden trees, the pond with tall waving grasses that bordered the property, and the traditional quadrant-style eight-acre garden that was conceived by the first owners in 1916. "We both knew the instant we drove onto the property that this was the one. I could have bought it on the spot without even getting out of the car," she said.

The couple purchased the property and closed the contract on June 20, 1994—their twenty-fourth wedding anniversary. "It was a gift we gave to each other, and it was also a gift to our children. We wanted them to have memories of warm, carefree summers that they could dream about all year and remember all their lives," says Joan. During the next five years the home and gardens were refurbished to accommodate family and visiting friends, and the old bathhouse adjacent to the swimming pool was razed and replaced with a new pool house.

Joan visited the conservatories at Dumbarton Oaks in Washington, the New York Botanical Garden, and various conservatories in England. Inspired by these designs, she determined that she would like the new pool house to recall an orangery from another era.

A difficult space to renovate, it was confined on two sides by the pool and tennis court; both environmental and historical considerations forbade increasing the structure's size. "It wasn't a very large space, and yet we wanted men's and women's dressing rooms, proper seating, and a wet bar area, so we really had to use our imaginations to make it everything we wanted," says Joan. Clever architectural and design solutions included trompe l'oeil to create an illusion of equal wall proportions, two walls of windows, and glass doors that expose an entire wall to the outside to increase light and spaciousness. A ceiling of cut decorative glass framed with hand-painted sky and clouds evokes the outdoors and creates a bridge between inside and out. To emphasize the indoor garden effect the Carls wanted, antique mirrors were installed to reflect the exterior white gardens beyond, and treillage was fitted over the mirrors to suggest an inviting peek into the gardens beyond.

Locating authentic conservatory accessories and furnishings involved months of searching and traveling. A turn-of-the-century handcrafted wicker chaise, found in an antique store in Florida, and Bielecky cane chairs and an

The new pool house
would have the ambience
of an orangery from
another era.

*An extravagant basket of hydrangeas
vies with the sofa's rhododendron-print
Scalamandre fabric for attention.*

ottoman were covered in a Scalamandre pink-and-green rhododendron-print fabric that evoke the garden's extensive collection of mature rhododendrons. Two English watercolors purchased from a Washington, D.C., art dealer depict scenes of eighteenth-century orangeries, and hang as a reminder of the success and beauty of this twenty-first-century re-creation.

Filled with cascading, spiky ferns, a pair of late-nineteenth-century English clover–designed lead planters sit on a shelf above built-in love seats. Large wire baskets, purchased from the tony conservatory shop Marston and Langinger in London, hang from the ceiling and overflow with exuberant Boston ferns. Tiered, black-wire corner units, purchased on the same shopping trip, flank a door, brimming over with begonias in soft salmon color and lush greens. Majesty palms in huge clay pots give height to the luscious indoor landscape.

Views of the meticulously landscaped formal garden help to establish the interior mood. "I wanted continuity of the gardens and the pool house," Joan says, "and that makes the views of the garden very important." Vistas give

glimpses of Coopersneck Pond with swans gliding gracefully along the water. A swimming turtle, more than one hundred years old, pokes his head above the water, and a large female laboriously lays tracks along the lawn in search of a place to lay her eggs. Seven-foot-tall *Phragmites* grasses brought to the Hamptons by the original settlers grow densely along the shore and wave in the afternoon breeze.

The back windows overlook a queenly weeping beech, at fifty feet tall with a spread of almost eighty feet, its huge overhanging branches brushing the ground like a giant hoop skirt. The dappled interior is fitted with a miniature hammock, the family calls it the hiding tree, and by custom reserves it as a secret hideaway for children only.

Looking through the front glass doors, one sees an aqua blue swimming pool that serves as a frame for a seemingly boundless stretch of lawn and a white garden. The icy silver and white of roses, lantanas, pentas, hydrangeas, heliotrope, and verbena lends a soft elegance to the late morning; under a full moon the blossoms shine like tiny sparkling lights.

The Carls became the seventh owners of the property

in a line of family and garden loving residents. "This home has always represented family to everyone who has owned it, and every one of us has been a garden lover too," says Joan. In deference to the second owners, Doris and Robert Magowan, the Carls decided to revive their name for it, "Little Orchard."

The large, sunny home extends its inviting porches like embracing arms, with upholstered, sink-into furniture and a comfortable, welcoming character. "This was never meant as a big showy home, it was always intended as a family home," says Joan. "There were lots of guest rooms when we bought it, and we added more. I don't think a day goes by in the summer when we don't have at least fourteen people for dinner, and we are only a family of five. And this goes to the history of the house and the former owners too."

Guests are often invited to enjoy the lush environment at the pool house for drinks before dinner or coffee afterward. "We can barely see the stars in Washington, and so I am still amazed that we can sit out there and look up to the night sky and see the Little Dipper and the Big Dipper and every single constellation so clearly," says Joan. This is a space that family and friends frequent all day. The early morning, before the sun heats up the day and evaporates the dew, is another favorite time. "We often go out very early and have our breakfast there. It is so quiet, and we can see the quail, bunny rabbits, mother and baby deer bounding across the property, and it is really beautiful. The sprinklers come on, and even that is beautiful."

The sounds of nature that drift into the pool house from the garden are as arresting as the beautiful sights. The soft hushing of the ocean a block away, the gentle rustling of tall pond grasses, and the fluttering leaves on the beech trees harmonize with the flickering movements of birds, rabbits, and other tiny garden creatures. The water music of a fountain inside the pool house, made from a nineteenth-century English cistern, trickles rhythmically and adds to the relaxation. "The sounds of nature are so lovely here. We have a music system, and although I usually love to be surrounded by music, when I am in the pool house I'd rather be listening to nature. I honestly don't think I've turned on the music more than once or twice," says Joan.

Perhaps the most endearing music is that made by people. "There can either be the great peace and quiet of nature or a lot of very happy noise of the pets, friends, and children in the pool laughing and having fun," says Joan. The family's five cats, four dogs, and a parakeet add to the commotion, traveling with them from Washington to South Hampton. "We don't do business out here ever, so it is only a place for happy sounds and lots of laughter."

"It is both peaceful and very energizing to be in this lovely room," Joan adds. "Sometimes I come out here alone to read, and I find that it energizes me in a way I never realized I could be energized. As a mother especially, I feel so fortunate to have this happy place for our family."

The side patio entrance, a quiet retreat, looks out to the pond with its rustling grasses.

How Does Your Child's Garden Grow?

AS THE NURSERY RHYME SUGGESTS, your child's garden may grow with "silver bells and cockle shells, and pretty maids all in a row," but there are lots of other options. Many of the most talented gardeners got their start kneeling beside their parents or grandparents, inhaling the earthy fragrance and making beautiful things come to life. Teaching your child to garden can be a wonderful experience, guaranteed to make lifetime memories.

A secret or private little place in the home that your child can cultivate with you is a fun way to encourage pride and build self-esteem. Make a grouping of pots on a sunny windowsill in their bedroom or kitchen, and place a sign with the child's name on it. Provide your child with miniature tools and a watering can.

Children can help paint and decorate the pots and personalize them with their names. Stimulate their imaginations by letting them use unique planters like a plastic toy dump truck, or Dad's old sneaker. Keep them enthusiastic by not being too exacting—and remember, the fun is in the process. Remind them to always use fertilizer and pesticide products that are organic and healthy to be near.

Make them smile by planting food they can eat, like lettuce or herbs, which can easily be grown on a windowsill. Make an occasion of eating the crop your child has grown. Invite in some friends or grandparents to enjoy the salad your child grew; make a centerpiece from handpicked flowers and mint tea made from the herb garden.

Few plants will survive neglect like succulents, which include members of the cactus family. Starting with plants that don't require too much care helps to avoid discouragement.

Try some fun projects from things that cost little or nothing that can be found in your own home and will help to teach a child respect for the environment and the benefits of recycling. You can grow coffee, almonds, avocado plants, dates, or oranges by planting seeds or stones.

• Plant an avocado stone by pressing the round end into a pot filled with moist multipurpose soil. Keep in a warm place until the stone splits and a growth spike appears. Keep the compost moist as leaves develop and pinch out growing shoots to encourage bushiness. Repot annually, and in a few years the plant will be up to five feet tall. Unfortunately, it will not bear fruit.

• Plant a pineapple by cutting off the top inch of a ripe, fresh pineapple. Cut away the flesh to leave the leafy crown and fibrous core and allow it to dry out for a few days on a sunny windowsill. Plant in a pot filled with moist multipurpose soil and put in sunny spot to allow the root system to develop. Be careful not to overwater.

• A coffee bean can be grown into a healthy, bushy plant that will grow up to five feet tall, which will flower but not produce coffee beans. Use the beans from Coffea arabica or Coffea nana (available through vendors or catalogues that sell seeds), which flower more easily. Place in a small two-inch-deep pot with moist multipurpose

A crested mutation forms a living sculpture on this Arrojodoa rhodantha from Brazil.

soil, and set in a bright spot without direct sun. In a couple of weeks the plant will emerge. The plant must be kept free from drafts, and compost must be kept moist all the time. It should be repotted once it becomes root bound into a four-inch pot and repotted every spring.

Children love plants that do something.

• Peanuts or groundnuts (*Arachis hypogaea*) are easy to grow, and fascinating for children to watch. In the early spring remove the husk from an unsalted, raw peanut and plant it two inches deep in rich, moist compost. Keep watered and put in a well-lit warm spot. The plant will grow and bloom for a few hours, then wilt when self-pollination occurs. The flower stalk then lengthens and bends down to the ground, burrowing into the compost to begin the process of ripening.

• A Venus's-flytrap (*Dionaea muscipula*) is an unusual and entertaining carnivorous plant that eats insects. When the hapless creature lands on the hinged leaves, they snap shut and are digested by the plant for nutrients. It is a demanding plant, but endlessly fascinating to children. The Venus's-flytrap needs a bright, cool, damp place, and does best if placed in small container of water.

Above all, make gardening a pleasurable project that teaches patience and appreciation of aesthetic beauty, and one that encourages laughter and serenity. The gift of gardening will bring your children a lifetime of joy and stimulate sweet memories throughout their lives.

A list of additional projects and plants to grow with children is in the Appendix.

CHAPTER

THREE

❦

*Rare and
Delightful Home
Collections*

*I*t may be Wheaties boxes or Gauguins, Dresden figurines or hubcaps, valuable sculpture or baseball cards, cacti, orchids, or tropicals—but one thing is certain: when a collector finds the thing that touches his passion, there is a danger it might triumph over reason. Catherine the Great, Petrarch, Brunelleschi, and John Steinbeck were all obsessive about their acquisitions.

Collections can be displayed with reverence on walls or pedestals or simply boxed in a basement, giving the owner the sweet satisfaction of possession. One eccentric collector in California used millions of bottles amassed over the years as material for a lifesize backyard hamlet of thirteen buildings and twenty sculptures, including a six-foot Tower of Pisa constructed from milk of magnesia bottles.

Amateur plant collectors have contributed greatly to botanical research. Some have discovered plants thought previously extinct, while others have developed cultivars that changed the face of a whole plant family. Plant collection is a wildly popular hobby, as witness the thousands of international, national, and local plant societies focused on everything from fungi to orchids.

Most collectors are satisfied simply to possess the objects of their ardor. Plant collectors, however, must also nurture, cultivate, propagate, and cherish their charges. Many consider them friends, and it is no secret that some owners claim the plants they talk to thrive the best.

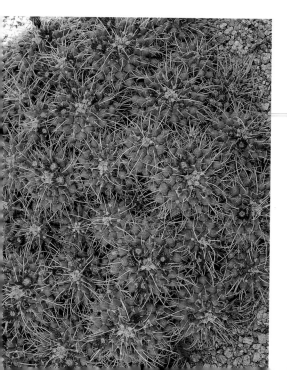

Previous spread: Cacti and other desert plants can be surreal in their sculptural beauty.

Far left: The low-growing cactus Echinocereus scheeri *has beautiful pink flowers and thin spikes.*

Left: The Iron Cross begonia, Begonia masoniana, *has boldly marked and textured leaves.*

Facing page: Given a perfectly controlled environment and careful nurturing, Kit Pannill's collection is an orchid lover's heaven.

Scottsdale Magical Desert

As the Spanish scribe and explorer Cabeza de Vaca explained on first seeing America's deserts in 1536, "Of all the things I have seen, this is the one that has left me without hope of being able to describe it in words." These words come easily to mind after a visit to the Scottsdale gardens of H. B. and Jocelyn Wallace.

Home to a wonderland of prickly, eccentric desert plants from all over the world, the one-of-a-kind 6,000-square-foot indoor desert garden pavilion indeed defies description. It is not only the sheer size of the indoor garden, with its stone-lined serpentine pathways that make you forget you are inside, its fifteen-feet-high movable louvered ceiling, and its immense glass walls, but also the private botanical collection itself that astonishes. "This is one of the most significant and finest desert plant collections we know of," says Richard Felger, botanist and executive director and founder of the Drylands Institute.

Facing page: Desert plants are some of Earth's most exotic and beautiful living sculptures.

Right: H. B. Wallace, a devoted desert conservationist, with friends.

Above: A crowd of columnar cacti jostle or space in the pavilion.

Right: A pink-flowered prickly pear,
Opuntia auberi, *leans against the thick trunks of the organ-pipe cactus* (Stenocererus thurberi); *the slender gray-spined stems behind them belong to the cactus* Lophocereus gatesii.

H. B., a spirited eighty-five-year-old conservationist and a passionate gardener, has dedicated the last sixteen years to creating this desert masterpiece and protecting the natural desert beyond it. He and Jocelyn purchased the property and began building the indoor pavilion and developing the garden in 1986, before the plan for their new home was complete.

The original idea was to have a one-acre garden, but that didn't last long. "I guess I just don't do things in little ways. Things have to start small, but by golly they don't have to stay small," said H. B. Two years later the eleven-acre botanical garden and pavilion were well on the way to housing one of the most extensive private desert collections in the world.

Designed by H. B., the state-of-the-art building is the first of its kind ever constructed. The object was to develop an indoor environment where nonhardy desert plants from all over the world, many rare and unique, would not only survive but also thrive in the Arizona climate.

The adobe-colored wood-and-metal-frame pavilion, set adjacent to the home site, was designed to meld into the natural desert landscape. Large ceiling louvers and special curtains open and shut, electrically powered, to control desert chill. Overhead gas heaters come on automatically when the temperature drops below 34 degrees Fahrenheit.

The pavilion has more than 250 cold-sensitive desert species from the deserts and dry tropics all over the globe, and the outdoor botanical garden has many more thousands of species. Five full-time employees are needed to maintain the gardens.

Here a visitor can contemplate the sculptural shapes, texture, and varied hues of plants with bizarre shapes, no leaves, and flowers that don't last more than a few hours. It's also a place to let your imagination run wild. Take, for instance, *Lophocereus schotti,* a treelike cactus from Mexico with shaggy manes and twisted spines that evolved to protect the tender young buds. The ten-foot multitrunked plant, by virtue of its white tufts that resemble an aging beard, is known as "old man of the desert" by the locals.

Another, the Brazilian *Arrojadoa rhodantha,* stands nine feet tall; fuzzy segments serve as markers of its age, and a head-size squiggly growth sprouts from it like oozing green toothpaste. Fine white fibers surround the spines of the huge *Cephalocereus* sp. from the lowlands of Brazil. Developed to protect it from the searing sun, they look like matted old lady's hair, stuck in a prickly hairbrush. A petite

Exotic, sometimes otherworldly, and always beautiful, it is also an important collection because of the educational opportunities it offers.

CYPHOSTEMMA
JUTTAE

Opuntia amuses with wiggling arms that reach along the sandy floor, and a *Pachycereus* with giant spiky humanoid arms outstretches to the sky and beckons with a menacing hug. One of the original acquisitions fifteen years ago, *Alluaudia procera* from Madagascar stands twenty-five feet tall, with many Medusa-like snaky branches.

One of the rarest and strangest plants is the *Welwitschia* sp. Three inches tall with two leaves, it hails from the Nabib desert in Africa. It will have only two leaves for all of its life, each of which could grow up to twenty feet long. This plant could live 500 to 1,000 years.

Exotic, sometimes otherworldly, and always beautiful, the Wallaces' collection is also important because of the educational opportunities it offers. Although the garden is private now, it was developed with an aim toward education and appreciation for desert plants. The University of Arizona uses it as a testing garden for various legumes at that elevation. Botanists, graduate students, and others interested in horticulture frequently tour. Recent guests were experts from the University of Iowa and Supreme Court Justice Sandra Day O'Connor.

"This collection is especially important because plants are in a natural environment outside, or inside in the pavilion, which simulates their natural environment. They are not in a greenhouse, and many can grow to their natural sizes. That not only makes it beautiful, but allows us to view a tiny slice of biodiversity that we would never be able to see without traveling all over the globe," says Dr. Felger.

H. B. has a special respect for the unique beauty of desert plants: "Oh, they are different, all right, and even though they are beautiful, they can be very mean." The octogenarian, who hikes in the desert several hours every morning with his three dogs, has the browned, leathery legs of an outdoorsman but hasn't escaped the stings of his prickly friends. "I haven't worn a pair of long pants in twenty years, and I have the scars and scrapes to prove it," he laughs.

A retired geneticist and successful breeder of Hy-Line chickens, H. B. left his Iowa home and extensive gardens in West Des Moines and moved west. Not a stranger to horticulture, he had one of the largest and most renowned gardens in Iowa. With rolling lawns and acres of vegetable, annual, and perennial beds, including hundreds of dahlias, his garden was said to be bigger than the one at the State House. "I've always been a gardener," he says. "I was a kid who grew wildflowers and a teenager who raised corn. I've always wanted to watch things grow. It's not even the flowers really, I just want to see things grow."

Facing page: The desert plants in the Wallace gardens are from all over the world.

Right: The exterior of the Wallace Botanical Garden pavilion is landscaped with a selection of plants that do well in the Arizona desert.

Above, from left to right: The low-growing cactus Echinocereus scheeri; *a crested mutation makes a living sculpture of this* Myrtillocactus geometrizans; *the starvation prickly pear,* Opuntia macrocentra *var.* macrocentra.

Facing page: These giants tower over smaller species. The gardeners find it is necessary to top the twenty-five to thirty heads a year that reach the fifteen-foot ceiling.

When H. B. moved to Arizona in the early 1980s, it was to escape the Iowa winter and enjoy sunshine all year, but what he encountered was a fascinating new aspect of gardening: "When you get into several thousand different species of plants from the deserts of the world, that's a whole lot more interesting than an Iowa vegetable garden."

During the 1980s the Wallaces began purchasing large parcels of desert land. With an eye to protecting the delicate ecosystem of the surrounding desert and fending off encroaching development, they established a seventy-eight-acre preserve of desert and mountain area. "I haven't always been a conservationist, it was something I didn't think about much before I moved here from Iowa, but I became deeply concerned that the desert and all the beautiful plants were being taken over with development. I knew if something wasn't done, it would be gone forever." The Wallace Botanical Garden Foundation was created, and an endowment established to assure continued resources for maintaining the pristine desert environment.

An additional twenty-five acres that includes the private botanical garden, pavilion, and home will continue to be available for educational purposes and eventually be maintained by the endowment as well. "We have a responsibility to pay attention not only to our own future but to the future of other generations too. We need to leave more than miles and miles of houses," says H. B.

Contributing to community welfare is not new to the Wallace family. H. B. is a geneticist like his father, H. A. Wallace, who was vice president of the United States under President Franklin Roosevelt and Progressive Party presidential candidate in 1948. Jocelyn is a descendent of George Washington, and both have a deep commitment to bettering their community. Says H. B. "I'm eighty-five years old now, and I still plan to live a very long time. But I think if we can eventually leave something that will continue to help others for a long time, then we will have done something really worthwhile. It's my hope that this will be here for hundreds and hundreds of years."

Growing Succulents Indoors

IMAGINE THE IDEAL PLANT THAT THRIVES ON NEGLECT, prefers poor soil, seldom wants to be watered, and has enough varieties to fill up every room in a hacienda, and you'll be envisioning a succulent. Their uniquely sculptural forms, sometimes bizarre appearance, large, colorful blossoms, and adaptability make them a welcome and easy-to-care-for addition to any indoor garden.

Succulents are clever plants; having adapted to harsh conditions by storing water in their leaves and stems, they need very little supplemental moisture to survive. Most succulents are terrestrial and live in sandy, well-drained soil. Some, however, are epiphytes that attach themselves in the wild to trees or rocks, receive the little water they need from the air, and require no soil at all to live.

Because many succulents, especially cacti, are so architecturally interesting, they make wonderful living sculptures. An interior desertscape can be simulated to create an attractive look in your home. A rotund barrel cactus, stately saguaro, or large euphorbia placed in a corner, or against a mirror to increase both light and effect, can be a dramatic backdrop. *Sedum morganianum* (donkey's tail), *Senecio rowleyanus* (string-of-beads), and *Ceropegia woodii* (rosary vine) all have long trailing habits that make beautiful hanging plants.

One of the best ways to assure that you choose a healthy plant is to purchase it from a reputable nursery or mail-order company. Look for the healthiest plant, not the biggest. Give it a gentle tug to know that it is well rooted and check to see that it doesn't have scarred or broken leaves or pests such as mealybug or scale. Check a plant carefully before introducing it to the rest of your collection.

We can take our cue from nature about how to care for most succulents. For transplanting, a good soil mixture is one part coarse sand, available at a builder's supply company, and two parts sterile compost. Commercial mix is also available at most garden centers. A top dressing of pebbles or crushed rock will give it a finished appearance, prevent the soil from becoming crusty, and help to retain a little moisture. Remove spiky cacti from pots by wrapping a newspaper, folded into a narrow strip, around the plant and lifting it out of the pot using the newspaper edge as a handle.

Facing page, left and right: These more delicate desert plants contrast with their hardy cousins on the exterior.

Container culture for succulents is easy, but there are some tips that will help to encourage success. Because potted plants are limited in their access to food and moisture, they will require more light, more water, and more frequent applications of fertilizer than those planted in the garden. There is no set rule about how often to water succulents because it depends on the light intensity, temperature, and moisture in the room, but most prefer to dry out a little between waterings.

Most succulents have high light requirements and do best in bright light with some direct sun. Good placement might be a sunny southern or western window. There are a few exceptions, however, so check a plant's requirements before placing it in your home. Many hawthornias and epiphyllums, for example, require more moderate light. Supplemental lighting with units especially designed for cultivating plants can also be an option if natural window light is limited. (See appendix A, p. 148.)

Good air circulation will help to prevent some pests like spider mites. Keep air moving with an open window, and resist the temptation to collect more plants than you have room to accommodate. Allowing air to become stagnant in a room is a sure way to entice unwanted critters.

For a list of interesting succulents to grow indoors, see appendix B, p. 155.

HOUSTON FISH TALE

TRUE TO THEIR TEXAS SPIRIT, WHEN THIS HOUSTON COUPLE decided to build a koi pond and mini jungle adjacent to their living room, they did it in a very big way.

Meet Beth and Bruce Grunden, who call this unique and serene environment home. When the Grundens purchased their property in 1978, it had a tiny pond with a few ferns around it in the entryway. When they moved in, in the fall of that year, a single koi was swimming in the pond, abandoned by the former owner. "We were so intrigued by that little fish, and things just really got carried away," said Beth.

"Carried away" is an understatement. Twenty-four years later the Grundens, with more than thirty prizewinning koi, are nationally known experts and have garnered more than fifty major awards, including the prestigious SoCal ZNA Twenty-sixth Open Koi Show Grand Champion Award. Home for their koi is a 1,500-square-foot tropical oasis with an almost 15,000-gallon pond, stone waterfalls, a variety of rare jungle plants, and the natural fragrance of a rain forest. And it's all indoors.

Facing page: A sturdy dining table and chairs offer comfort for family dining and koi viewing.

A pond with fish needs to look natural. The idea was to bring the outside in and the koi and plants go hand in hand.

The Grundens' beloved Koi enjoy the lush indoor garden room that was built especially for them and the surrounding tropical plants.

In 1997 the Grundens retired and decided to fulfill a long-held dream to renovate their garden and build an indoor conservatory. When the half-acre property next door became available for sale, they decided to purchase it. The project, which involved tearing down the house next door, incorporating and renovating the new space, and building the new conservatory, took more than two years.

The glass-encased garden room the Grundens designed was outfitted with state-of-the-art equipment to maintain the tropical plants and prize koi. The result is an indoor tropical paradise that houses an extensive collection of tropical and desert plants. A giant white bird-of-paradise *(Strelitzias nicolai)*, fishtail palm *(Caryota* sp.) and coconut palm *(Cocos nucifera)* loom overhead, creating a protective canopy for the assortment of exotic orchids, cycads, palms, and other unusual plants with colorful common names like the pregnant onion, elephant's foot, tapeworm plant, per-

fume tree, and Mickey Mouse plants. Rare flowering succulents, night-blooming cereus, staghorn ferns in decorative planters, and an ant plant hanging from the ceiling add to the jungle mood. A mango *(Mangifera indico)* and several varieties of banana trees might even provide a snack as one strolls through the indoor garden.

"Even the most jaded plant collector would have to be impressed with the plants the Grundens have in their conservatory," says Michael Lowery, a rare plant specialist from Another Place in Time Nursery in Houston. "The room is ideal because it has several microclimates, and that enables them to grow plants that would usually require completely different climate conditions." Desert-dwelling agaves, aloe, and yuccas share the conservatory with tropical heliconia, birds-of-paradise, and many varieties of orchid. "It's amazing because they all live together in that room," says Michael.

The air circulation, lighting, and temperature, the controlled humidity from the pond, and the care the Grundens lavish on their plants also help to make it successful. A vanilla orchid, which climbs up a west-facing wall, gets the afternoon sun and has new clusters of tiny white-and-yellow buds waiting to burst open. "It is very hard to get that plant to bloom, and it took a few years, but they've managed to do it. Like so many of the other plants there, it just has a great environment and some very good care," Michael says.

Tons of giant mossy green boulders, every crevice planted with orchids, bromeliads, and lush ferns, mounded as if by nature's hand, create a trickling waterfall that feeds into the shadowed waters. Bruce, who was moved as a child by the musical sounds of nature, wanted to rekindle the memory. "There are few sounds to me that are as soothing or as comforting as moving water. We have water features all over the house and garden, but in the garden room I wanted to remember the sounds of a babbling brook like the one I remember as a child, so I decided to re-create it."

Fifteen show-quality koi live in the interior environment, which emulates their natural habitat, and another fifteen champions live in specially constructed waterways in the exterior garden. Patterns of red, white, and black flash through the dark water, and round yawning mouths nip at the surface. Big Bertha, a thirty-inch champion from Japan, is the first to snap up tossed food bits and rules the water. Madame Butterfly, a shy and graceful sixty-two-pound, thirty-five-inch beauty who likes to be hand-fed, is the SoCal grand champion. "They are more than champions to us. I walk along the pond, and they follow me; some will only eat out of my hand. They are really pets with unique and individual personalities. To this day they still amaze me," says Beth.

"The garden room was built as a framework for our tropical plant collection and the koi," says Bruce. "A pond with fish needs to look natural. The idea was to bring the outside in, and the koi and plants go hand in hand."

Both received their Master Gardener certificates, but the couple arrived as avid plant collectors via different routes. Bruce, whose mother was president of her garden club and a flower-show judge, was indoctrinated early: "We'd drive down the highway as kids with my mom, and she'd point out every plant on the side of the road and teach us all the Latin names." From an early age he and his brother helped tend the flower and vegetable gardens and

Above: This lead statue adds an Asian flavor to the rubber plants, ferns, and bromeliads in the background.

Below: The dark leaves of the begonia 'Maurice Amey' set off the eccentric florescence of an Aechmea *sp. bromeliad.*

reveled in the wild turtles, frogs, and other small creatures that lived near the family's two-acre New Jersey home. In contrast, Beth was a garden spectator in her Milwaukee childhood. "I hardly ever saw the gardener who took care of our garden," she admits, laughing.

Today, however, the couple's passion for rare and unusual plants is mutual. "I love the oddball stuff," says Bruce. "I love cycads. They were here with the dinosaurs, and they fascinate me." For her part, Beth is intrigued with the rare and beautiful vine that climbs up the northern wall. "The vanilla orchid was planted four years ago, and until this year had only vegetative growth. I can't explain the excitement when we started getting these beautiful orchid blooms this year. It is truly a wonderment."

Specialists from Dallas who design commercial arenas were brought in to consult on the unusually large home project. The twenty-foot ceiling, equipped with six eight-by-eight-foot screened polycarbonate window bays, is designed to retract, powered by electrical motors. A specially designed pump system filters all 15,000 gallons of water every hour. Essential for maintaining healthy koi, a three hundred square foot room was built to house the massive pump system. A chiller maintains the pool temperature below 77 degrees Fahrenheit during the hot summer months; special fans and a climate control system keep the water and room environment operating at peak performance.

Rex Wilroy, a fellow koi hobbyist who helped build the pond, was impressed not only by the size of the project but by the Grunden's contributions and leadership. "These are very dedicated people," he says. "Beth started one of the local koi clubs, and they have won lots of awards, but the awards are not what motivate the Grundens. They really want to give back. They could win every competition if they wanted to, but honestly they don't. They want others to win so the pleasure of raising koi will be appreciated. They are really exceptional people in that way."

The Grundens wanted an extension to their home that was informal and comfortable for their children and granddaughter. Chocolate-colored flagstone floors, sturdy, comfortable furniture, and a built-in bar set the stage for a room built to be enjoyed. Family meals are usually taken there. Beth and Bruce often sit and relax at the end of the day with refreshment and feed the fish or tend the plants. It is also a spot to entertain and invite friends or hold committee meetings for one of their many charity involvements. One memorable event was a pre-wedding party for friends, with 200 guests; another was a barbeque with a full jazz band. "Some of our parties have lasted until five in the morning. It's a place to have great fun and make good memories. People come, and it feels so good in there that they just don't want to leave."

From a personal perspective, it is also a place for renewal and peace. "It is the most calm and serene place on earth. Building this room was one of the best things we've ever done," says Beth. "It's become a retreat in our own home. I'm not a religious person, but it's so filled with life and spirit here. And it's a heck of a lot better than $300 an hour for therapy."

Vanilla planifolia *is the only orchid that grows on a vine. The vanilla "bean" is actually an orchid seedpod.*

Gardening without Soil

HYDROPONICS, A METHOD OF GROWING PLANTS WITHOUT SOIL, can be a clean, convenient, and fun method of growing vegetables, fruit, and ornamentals all year, indoors. If fresh homegrown tomatoes, crunchy peppers, juicy peaches, and sweet apricots in the dead of winter are an appealing thought, hydroponics might be for you.

Hydroponics allows plants to live the good life. Instead of laboring to extract nutrients and water from the soil, they are fed like royalty with a silver spoon. A plant grown hydroponically is given, in place of soil, a nutrient-rich solution of fertilizer and water, which is misted, flooded, or pumped into the root system. The result is a plant that grows faster and more vigorously and produces more.

Although the number of people using hydroponics in their homes has skyrocketed since the 1970s, the process has been around for thousands of years. The Egyptians gardened hydroponically, and the Aztecs in Central America planted on floating rafts. Ancient Chinese boat dwellers hung gardens off their boats and grew vegetables on rivers and lakes, and the Hanging Gardens of Babylon are considered to have been hydroponic. The method is high-tech, too: NASA scientists grow vegetables hydroponically in space stations.

Gardening hydroponically at home can be as simple as forcing a hyacinth in a bulb vase with water or as involved as a fully automated, dedicated room with state-of-the-art lighting, pumps, and tanks that support all the homegrown fruits and vegetables for a growing family.

Simply, the method involves washing soil from the roots of plants and placing them in containers with a sterile medium like pebbles, glass beads, clay aggregate, or vermiculite to support the roots. The container is filled with a special solution of nutrients and water, and artificial lighting, heat, and ventilation is provided to simulate natural elements and the sun.

Indoor gardeners love it because it is cleaner—weed, disease, and pest free. Fruits and vegetables can be grown without toxins or pesticides. Crops can be harvested all year, regardless of the season, and boast considerably larger yields than with traditional gardening. A hydroponic system, properly managed, should produce at least a 20 to 25 percent increase in yields of tomatoes, cucumbers, pepper, and lettuce, for example. Hydroponics requires less space than soil gardening, and enables a large selection of ornamental plants as well as fruits and vegetables to be grown in very small spaces.

This Asian-style bonsai container is planted with fittonia, ferns, and silver-leafed syngonium. The miniature garden ornament is an antique Buddha figurine.

Hydroponic gardening also has some disadvantages. Initially it can be costly to construct a sophisticated hydroponic garden, but eventually the costs will be made up in food production, time, and savings on outdoor gardening. It also requires some vigilance, and although it takes less time in general, the system must be checked on a regular basis. Third, hydroponics can become a delightfully addictive pastime.

If this method of raising plants interests you, start on a small scale. Small, inexpensive units are available at specialty stores and on-line. The public library will also have information.

For a list of plants for starting a hydroponic garden, see appendix B, p. 155 .

PALM BEACH ORCHIDACEOUS

ENTER THE ARCHITECTURAL GEM that is the core of this waterfront Palm Beach garden, and cross into a burgeoning wonderland of exotic and mysterious plants that amaze and delight, including several hundred vanda, cattleya, dendrobium, and brassia orchids, as well as cacti and other succulents. When I visited they were at their spring finest, in full blossom in a pristine white slat house.

The proprietors of this bit of indoor Eden are Kit and Bill Pannill. In 1985 the couple retired, moved to Palm Beach from Virginia, and purchased a British colonial waterfront home on Lake Worth. Designed in 1950 by renowned Palm Beach architect John Volk, it had large, gracious rooms and an airy open-air floor plan but was in disrepair. Nevertheless, the Pannills knew immediately it would be home. "I fell in love with it because it was a comfortable, old-fashioned house that reminded me of home in Virginia."

Left: Kit Pannill admires Vanda 'Kit Pannill,' *an orchid named in her honor by the American Orchid Society.*

Facing page: The dramatic entrance to the slat house.

The trellis work is very English and provides
just the right environment for the orchids.

An important selling point was the expansive space available for planting. "We are both passionate about gardening, and it's one of the things we share and love," says Kit. Although modestly landscaped, the garden was graced with stately trees like the hundred-year-old *Ficus altissima* and fifty-foot *Ficus benjamina,* breathtaking views of the lake, and the skeletal makings of a great garden. They immediately began renovations on the home and planting the garden, building a notable collection of rarities. "Being unique is a key thing for me," Kit says, "and I think that is what really gives our garden character. We probably have one of the largest collections of unusual plants, both inside and outside, of anyone I know."

Five years after the Pannills moved in, the adjacent property became available. "Kit is an extraordinary gardener, and is always growing and in flux just like her garden. I knew it was just a matter of time before she ran out of space," her friend and interior designer Leta Austin Foster said, laughing. The Pannills purchased the next-door lot and doubled the size of their garden.

An important addition to the new garden, they decided, would be a structure to accommodate Kit's growing collection of orchids. Since the early days of tending a few orchids under plant lights in a small room in her Virginia home, Kit found that both her collection and her passion had grown. "I thought I'd just build a little wooden thing that wasn't too fancy. But Leta had different ideas and said, 'Oh, no, this has to be something really beautiful that everyone will see, a focal part for your yard.'"

Palm Beach architect Jacqueline Albarran was hired to design and draw the plans for the slat house. Her expertise was especially needed as a precaution against the 130-mile-an-hour Florida hurricane winds. "We all worked together," says Jacqueline. "Leta and Kit knew what they wanted, and we all put our heads together to make it a special place."

To ensure that the new slat house complemented the British colonial home, it was modeled after the Anglo-Indian architecture of the eighteenth and nineteenth centuries. With a swooping twenty-foot-high roof and fanciful rounded posts, arches, and columns, the slat house suggests a fabulous tent in the desert. "It reminds me of the almost decadent but amazing period of architecture under the British Raj when they built these incredible pleasure palaces," says Leta. "And of course the trellis work is very English and provides just the right environment for the orchids."

Facing page: The slat house duplicates the dappled sun that orchids receive in their natural environment.

Above: The beautiful Baldens's Kaelidscope *is admired for its creamy yellow and pink markings.*

Below: This Orthophytum gurkenii *has a beautiful color.*

Landscape architect Morgan Wheelock was called in for help in melding the old garden with the new and organizing the site. Kit worked alongside the landscapers to make sure every detail was perfect.

Darren Duling, director of horticulture at the American Orchid Society, testifies to Kit and Bill's dedication: "This is not a garden where someone came in and waved their hands and said, 'Okay, do it,' and then wrote a check. All the plants in the slat house are interesting and special to Kit, and every one in the garden was personally selected and positioned by her. Bill and Kit both actually get in there and work in their garden, and a lot of people in Palm Beach just don't do that. They are real gardeners."

Other specialists have also recognized their dedication and expertise. Kit has received two Catherine Beattie Medals from the Garden Club of America and has been honored by the American Orchid Society. Bill, an accomplished amateur daffodil hybridizer, has received awards from the Royal Horticulture Society and the American Daffodil Society. He was recently awarded the prestigious Amateur Hybridizer of the Millennium Award from the American Daffodil Society, and a medal has been named in

his honor, the William G. Pannill Award. His cultivar 'Intrigue,' one of the world's best-selling daffodils, received the award for Best Garden Flower.

The Pannills' commitment and enthusiasm shine through in their garden. Today pathways wind through the impeccably planted waterfront grounds, guiding visitors to the heart of the garden, the Lucite-lined slat house. Filled with hundreds of vibrantly colored orchids—all award winners—it is an astounding sight. Says Kit, "There are just too many orchids in the world and too little space not to have only the really special ones."

One of the centerpieces of the collection is a recent gift of an iridescent ivory-and-peach-colored orchid, *Vanda* 'Kit Pannill,' named in her honor by the American Orchid Society. Another namesake was born the same month; Kit's new granddaughter. "I just think it is a thrill of a lifetime to have these two great beauties named for me. And you know they actually look alike, so peachy and perfect," she said.

Masses of purples, magentas, yellows, oranges, whites, and reds blend to create a symphony of color and design against the many-hued tapestry of leaves and the stark white lines of slatted wood. Darren Duling was delighted when he visited, enthusing, "This place is a real showcase and is something you just don't see in private homes. It is also beautifully maintained and pristine with an amazing collection of the most healthy plants and bumper crop blooms."

Luminously green, ropelike roots hang from the ceiling in teak baskets, overflowing with multihued blossoms that move gently in the warm, fragrant tropical breeze. Dappled sunlight plays over benches crowded with precisely placed pots of orchids in full flower.

There is more to the collection than exotic beauty, however. Kit's collection of unusual cacti, succulents, and caudiciforms, with their odd, swollen forms, add additional interest and a bit of living sculpture to the mix. "My husband says the weirder and uglier they are, the more I like them," Kit jokes.

Designed to satisfy the aesthetics of the owners as well as to protect the plants, the slat house is a stylish and comfortable environment. The eight-hundred-square-foot structure was fitted with traditional Florida stone and brick floors. Special heaters were installed, coming on when the temperature drops below 50 degrees Farenheit to protect the cold-sensitive plants and to allow Kit to work in any weather. Fans assure proper ventilation, and shades can be adjusted to direct the light. A specially designed Lucite ceiling protects against driving tropical rains that can be harmful to some plants and a nuisance to people, while allowing the sun in. "It was important to me that it could be a place to relax, to enjoy and work with the plants and appreciate the surrounding gardens all year," says Kit.

The original idea for the slat house has changed since its inception. "I always imagined that in the middle of the room there would be a table and some lovely furniture where one could read or dine out among the orchids," says Leta. "But you know, the room took on a life of its own. Kit is passionate about her orchids, and she kept falling in love with new ones and filling up the room, and before we knew it the plants literally became more important than eating."

I asked Kit what drew her and others to orchids, and she told me, "I think people are so crazy about orchids not only because they are so immensely beautiful, but because they are so sensual and erotic looking. People find that when they get involved with them, it's sort of like eating a peanut. You can't eat just one."

Above: A close-up of the orchid Vanda 'Kit Pannill.'

Facing page: The white ruffles of these cattleya blooms also called Gladis Barton are set off by their dramatic yellow throats.

Below: These orchids are a Laeliocattleya *hybrid.*

Growing Orchids Indoors

ORCHIDS ARE MYSTERIOUS AND SENSUAL. They conjure up exotic rain forests, romance, and vacations in the tropics. They accompany the important occasions in our lives as christening flowers, prom corsages, wedding bouquets, and funeral wreaths.

Many indoor gardeners are intimidated by orchids, believing they are hard to grow and impossible to persuade to bloom. If you choose the right varieties and follow a few guidelines, however, orchids can be a satisfying hobby, and a gorgeous addition to your indoor garden.

Nearly all orchids live in the warm, moist climate of the rain forests of the world. In the wild most don't live in soil, but wrap their roots around the branches of trees. They belong to the class of plants called epiphytes, which are not parasitic but receive their water and nutrients from decaying matter that falls from the trees, rain, and the natural humidity in the air.

If we understand the conditions in which orchids thrive in the wild, we can then duplicate these, within reason, in our homes. Wood bark, rock wool, gravel, and even wine corks are often used for potting orchids, as most will suffocate in soil. They need a medium that will accommodate their air roots and simulate their natural environment, on the branches of trees.

Light and water requirements for orchids vary, but all require a combination of high humidity and good air circulation. Providing these things in the home takes awareness and a little ingenuity. Bathrooms and kitchens, often more humid than the rest of the house, are good places for orchids. Some growers use humidifiers hidden behind furniture, but if you do that you will want to protect floors, fabrics, and furniture, which may be damaged by dampness. Placing plants on trays lined with pebbles and water and grouping plants together are two excellent ways to increase humidity. Keep plants away from heating vents or other drying environments. Using a fan or simply opening a window will encourage air circulation, keeping plants insect- and disease-resistant.

If this is a new hobby, choose orchids that are easy to grow. The orchid family is the largest plant family in the world; with 25,000 species to choose from, finding the right one can be a challenge. Some of the most beautiful and agreeable to cultivate at home are the *phalaenopsis*, also called the moth orchid; the *paphiopedilum* or lady's slipper; the *cattleya*; and the *miltonia*. Each requires slightly different conditions, so there is certain to be one that will do well in your home.

A laeliocattleya hybrid *glows against dark foliage.*

The most common mistake of new orchid growers is killing them with kindness—overwatering, which causes root rot. In climates where drought can be a problem, many orchids have developed thickened water-storing stems called pseudobulbs to see them through dry spells. It is wise to inquire about the watering needs of each orchid you acquire.

Orchids are light feeders compared to other houseplants, so you will want to fertilize frugally. A buildup of whitish residue on the inner rim of the pot or on the roots is a sure sign you are overfeeding. An excellent—though foul-smelling—fertilizer for orchids is fish emulsion. Orchids love it, it is natural and chemical-free, and it leaves no salt residue.

Orchid blooms can last for months; they fill our surroundings with fragrance and stunning beauty, and have an extraordinary allure. Take caution if you are considering buying your first orchid. Collectors have been known to swoon for them, murder for them, and sell all their worldly possessions to acquire the one of their dreams. Be prepared to become addicted.

For a list of interesting orchids to grow indoors, see appendix B, p. 153.

CHAPTER

FOUR

❧

*City Living
and Agrarian
Comfort*

ity living generates vitality and energizes those who love it. Steel, glass and concrete can be a thing of exhilarating beauty, and museums, symphony, opera and theater add to the verve for urbanites who wouldn't live anyplace else. The same verve and hustles that energize, however, can also be depleting. Many wise city dwellers have discovered the antidote: a garden haven. Thriving plants fifty stories above the city streets— a living room filled with sweet-smelling orchids, a tiny kitchen herb box, or an unlikely tropical paradise in a small city bathroom—can be the ideal refuge.

An indoor garden in a city home, especially one that does not have outdoor space, will counter the stress of urban living and satisfy our craving to return to nature and our roots. These green sanctuaries improve our physical and mental health by freshening our air, lifting our spirits, and beautifying our lives.

Previous spread: A luminous conservatory seems to float in the darkness.

Facing page: Accessories can help accentuate an indoor plant grouping. Here, a delightful garden statue is nestled among miniature roses.

Right: Trailing ivy softens any planter, and the variegated leaf pattern adds interest and beauty.

New York Soaring Green Vistas

THE DIN OF TRAFFIC AND ODOR OF EXHAUST mingle incongruously with the gentle babbling of a fountain and the sweet fragrance of gardenias and jasmine. Fifteen stories above the bustle, this Park Avenue penthouse garden is an oasis in a cement city. An enclosed glass conservatory, planted with gardenias, hydrangeas, azaleas, jasmine, and dark green topiary, opens onto a circle of terraces that sweep around the apartment, where masses of crab apple blossoms, pendulous violet wisteria, and old-fashioned roses offer a verdant screen of city views.

The owners, who lived for many years in a large house with a mature garden in Westchester and now have a second home and garden in Connecticut, looked for many years for a New York apartment to replace their suburban home. Frequent attendees of New York's opera, theater, and concerts, they loved the vibrancy of city living but yearned to be surrounded by the calming elements of the country. "I am a passionate gardener and spend every waking moment in my Connecticut garden when I'm there. My husband complains that he sometimes has to come find me with a flashlight," laughs the wife.

Facing page: Azaleas, gardenias, and seasonal perennials help to soften the cityscape.

Above: Views of the city are screened by classical trelliswork, fruit trees, and overflowing planter boxes.

Below: Daisy and Megan, the family's West Highland terriers, find comfort in a sunny corner.

She remembers their first viewing in 1998 of the penthouse apartment that would become their new home, and her excitement at the possibility of building a conservatory on a section of the ample terrace: "The apartment was perfect in so many ways because we would be able to build a beautiful indoor space where I could garden all through the seasons, and have outdoor space too. You just don't find that in New York."

With panoramic views that stretch from the East River to the Chrysler Building, the Empire State Building, and Central Park, the wraparound outdoor terraces covered more square footage than the indoor apartment; the couple had met the almost impossible goal of finding a large open-air space in the middle of America's great metropolis. "I knew that even though I desperately wanted to live in the city, I wanted to be able to go outside from my apartment to garden. That narrowed our options considerably. I also knew I'd never leave my home until I found the perfect place—and we looked for fifteen years. But it was worth the wait."

Rosario Candela, a premier architect of grand New York apartment buildings, had designed the prewar building in 1926. "It had so much to offer—the outdoor space and views—and unlike some penthouses that were afterthoughts, with a makeshift quality, it was not only well built and sound, but also had very beautiful architectural details," says the wife, a New York stage actress and singer. The couple took almost two years to renovate the existing seven rooms and add an eighth, the conservatory.

New York architect Robert Stewart Burton was called in to design the classic dark green conservatory, and Amdega Conservatories provided the British-made components. Conforming to New York City's stringent regulations was at times difficult. It was not possible to bring in cranes to hoist materials, so landscape and building materials had to be brought up through the service elevators. "It was definitely not problem-free, but for one of the largest private conservatories in New York, building this was smoother than most. It was worth it, too, because they now have one of the most extensive roof gardens and most beautiful settings I've seen here in New York," says Brian Krapf, a representative of Amdega Conservatories.

New York landscape architect Halsted Welles was hired to design the exterior landscaping and to consult on the finishing touches and plantings in the new conservatory; as the owner explains, "I wanted someone who could do this

Left: The conservatory serves as a natural transition from the roof garden to the interior of the apartment. Raised paneling on the planters matches the paneling in the dining room.

very large-scale job; remember, there was absolutely nothing there. It was just an enormous space without so much as a plant or a pot, and everything had to be created from the beginning."

The outcome is a spectacular 2,000-square-foot roof garden, divided into garden rooms with dark green trellised panels. Trickling fountains, a landscaped hot tub room, and espaliered apple and pear trees help to create an air of luxury. An enchanting garden gate leads to a trellised pergola, an intimate, private space. Wisteria, roses, and tall pines frame the breathtaking exterior garden, seen from its entry, the conservatory.

The star of the garden is the 335-square-foot indoor space. "I think the success of this garden is how each space flows into another. The movement through the garden and into the conservatory is wonderful and a very important

element of it," says Halsted. "The conservatory gives one a vantage of the roof garden, and it is all-season gardening. It's about as close to outdoor living as us northeasterners get during the year."

Infused with the sweet fragrance of jasmine and gardenias, and crowded with vibrant seasonal planting such as hydrangeas, paperwhites, passionflowers, camellias, amaryllis, foxgloves, pansies, violas, and topiaries, the conservatory dazzles in every season. "I put votive candles on the windows with Christmas wreaths, narcissus, pines and amaryllis during the holidays. In the spring I have bulbs and foxgloves, and there are always annuals," says the owner. "It can have a different look and feel every season and it's always so lovely." The conservatory encourages new and unusual gardening too. "I can grow things that will do well in some warmer places in the country but are unheard of in

New York in the winter. I've ordered a lemon tree because it has that wonderful fragrance, and it will be such fun to have the fruit."

It is also a place to increase one's green-thumb confidence. "My gardenias are blooming now, and they are not that easy to grow here. It was just so exciting to see those buds. These were not mature plants I went and bought and put in the conservatory. They were very small, and I've nurtured them, so it is so satisfying to see them erupt with blossoms."

The owner also realized the importance of melding the look of the inside and out: "It was important to me that the new conservatory and outside terraces would make a good transition from the traditional interior of the apartment." Raised panels on the flower boxes were designed to match the raised paneling on the cabinetry inside, and fabric for the conservatory furniture was selected to blend with the formal Chinese wallpaper in the dining room. "I wanted everything to fit like a single piece, and look as if it belonged together and was always here together."

The antique wicker furniture was a serendipitous find in a small Connecticut antique shop: "I couldn't believe my eyes when I saw the furniture, it was exactly what I was looking for and there it was just waiting for me." In keeping with the design of the room, a Robert Kime hand-printed floral linen fabric was chosen to cover the furniture. The floor is terra-cotta-colored ceramic tile, chosen for its minimal upkeep. "The floor is impervious to almost anything, which is great because we are always hauling plants around; it gets wet and sometimes even a little muddy, so it was a very good decision."

Everyone gravitates to the conservatory. "In the middle of winter, on a cold, wet day, it is as warm as toast in there," says the owner. "It's just a place where everyone wants to be." Eighteen guests sit down here for a sunny Sunday brunch; grandchildren play; the family relaxes over a leisurely weekend breakfast; daily telephone calls are made; friends enjoy cocktails or gather for a peaceful afternoon visit over tea—it is the most enjoyed and used room in the apartment. "It's amazing, really. The conservatory wasn't even here when we bought the apartment, and now we can't imagine how we could have done without it."

Although its rewards are great, indoor gardening fifteen stories high is not without tribulations. Bags of soil, garden supplies, and pots of plants—not immune to spills—must all be carted up on the elevator, and trash must be hauled down. "It's more challenging than gardening in the backyard. It's not as easy as dashing off to the nursery to pick up a few things. My doorman must cringe every Sunday night when I come back from the country, because he knows I've got at least a few flats in the back of my car."

But, however impractical high-rise urban gardening may be, its pleasure more than compensates. "It is wonderful," says the owner. "This conservatory is truly a haven and a refuge. I love the city and everything that goes on in the city, but there is nothing like walking in here and feeling the peace and beauty of this wonderful place. It is truly my own private paradise."

Facing page: A favorite place for cozy family dinners. The owner says, "In the middle of winter on a cold, wet day it's just as warm as toast in here."

Making Terrariums and Wardian Cases

CONSIDER A FANTASY INDOOR GARDEN FOR A BUSY PERSON. Think of a lush landscape filled with exotic tropical and woodland plants. Imagine that it costs very little, rarely needs to be watered or fertilized, and is hardly ever bothered by pests; gazing at it transports you to a divine tropical vacation, and it fits neatly on the coffee table in your living room. It might sound too good to be true, but this dream could be a reality with a terrarium.

A terrarium is a garden with its own personal climate, a fascinating miniature replication of a natural jungle or woodland environment in a bottle, a fishbowl, a jar, an aquarium, or even a brandy snifter. Plants grown under glass practically take care of themselves, replenishing their own moisture through transpiration and manufacturing their own oxygen in a marvelous self-maintaining ecosystem.

Terrariums have been around since 500 B.C., when plants were cultivated under bell-shaped glass jars at the annual festival of Adonis in Greece. But not until the nineteenth century did the English physician Dr. Nathaniel Ward accidentally discover that plants could thrive for years in a sealed glass container. This development was to change the world of horticulture: although explorers and plant hunters of the day had been collecting rare and exotic specimens from all over the world, few plants had survived the long, harsh sea journey in good health. Protected in glass cases, however, camellias and banana trees from China, orchids from the Philippines, and cactus from America could be shipped safely to Europe. Terrariums and Wardian cases—ornate, elaborately carved pieces of furniture with glass cases fit inside—became the rage in European and American homes and few self-respecting Victorian parlors were without one.

Today terrariums are popular in modern homes because they are beautiful, fascinating, and require almost no maintenance. Terrariums allow the indoor gardener to grow a wide variety of plants that would not otherwise thrive in our dry, forced-air heated homes. They shield plants from drafts and abrupt temperature changes, conserve moisture and humidity, and admit necessary light.

A terrarium is easy and satisfying to make, and will give many years of pleasure. Almost any clean glass container, either clear or lightly tinted, that is large enough to accommodate plants and gives a full view of the interior can be used. If your home decor permits, an authentic Wardian case can be purchased for several thousand dollars, or a contemporary breakfront, armoire, or china cabinet can be converted into a modern-day version.

Left: Small tropical plants thrive in the Wardian case.

The container should be prepared with four layers of material before the plants are installed. Begin by creating a bottom layer for drainage in a two-gallon container, an inch of gravel at the bottom of the container. Build a second layer with a half inch of chipped or crushed charcoal to neutralize the fumes caused by decay in moist conditions. The third layer should be a fine covering of sphagnum moss to keep the soil on top from sifting through. Several layers of rich, sterilized potting soil make up the top layer. Mound the soil, with the higher side graduating toward the back of the container. All the layers together should fill the bottom fourth or fifth of the container.

Natural products like rocks or pieces of wood help to accent the landscape. Choose plants with varying heights, shapes, textures, and color, but with similar care requirements. Taller plants should be placed toward the back, with shorter plants toward the front and sides, and ground covers at the base. Insert plants starting with the tallest and work forward.

Choose plants that are slow-growing, miniature, or dwarf, and that will adapt well under glass. Some good choices for ground covers are baby's tears and most mosses. Smaller plants that do well are fittonia, devil's ivy, small-leafed English ivy, and peperomias. For taller plants consider calathea, Chinese evergreen, maidenhair fern, small-leafed philodendron, and small species of dracaena, dieffenbachia, palm, and umbrella plant.

Once you have finished planting, give a light watering with a spray bottle, aiming the water toward the sides of the case. Soil should be thoroughly wet, but not soaked. Allow leaves to dry for a few hours before replacing the lid. Put your terrarium in a well-lighted spot in your home, but not in the direct sun. Check daily to see that the humidity level is correct. If too much condensation has formed on the sides, remove the lid until it has dried. Check periodically, but do not water again unless the lid has been left off for an extended time and the soil has become dry.

For a list of additional plants for making a terrarium, see appendix B, p. 154.

GEORGETOWN HISTORIC GREENHOUSE

IF HOMES COULD TALK, THIS GEORGETOWN MANSION would reveal a fascinating story of the man who built it, the impact he had on the contemporary world, and the artist-designers who took residence when the family finally sold it, almost ninety years later.

The story would begin with an innovative inventor and engineer who was born during the Civil War. Herman Hollerith invented several things in his lifetime, but nothing else had the impact of his punch-card tabulation machine system, which led to the technology for computers. His company, Tabulating Machine Company, eventually became IBM. Hollerith's accomplishments are considerable. He was made a member of the Inventors Hall of Fame, and according to England's *Economist* magazine, his invention was one of the ten most important events in science and technology in the last thousand years.

Facing page: The newly renovated greenhouse offers wonderful views of the majestic garden beyond.

Right: Rob Brown and Todd Davis, with their dog, Madison.

Above: Miniature myrtles peek out from under the highly polished coffee table.

Facing page: This whimsical horse, a several-hundred-year-old import from India, was a find in a Georgetown antique shop.

By 1911, financially prosperous and with a large family, Hollerith decided to build a bigger home on his Georgetown property. Architect Frederick Pyle was hired to design the grand Georgian estate, the extensive gardens, and a state-of-the-art conservatory. Here he and his wife, Lucia Beverly, would raise their six children, and three of the children would live here for the rest of their lives.

Grandson Richard Hollerith spent spring vacations at his grandparents' home and recalls the grandeur of those days. "I remember sitting with the family for dinner, and there were always so many servants and we used fingerbowls and there were fresh flowers everywhere. The chauffeur took us out sightseeing in a long black limousine. I was just a little boy, but I knew that wasn't happening in many homes."

The several acres in the midst of Georgetown were an ideal site for Lucia's garden. A passionate and knowledgeable gardener, she was the founder and first president of the Georgetown Garden Club. Most of the specimen trees and shrubs in the landscape today were planted under her guidance.

The conservatory, attached to the house adjacent to the dining room, was fitted with the most up-to-date equipment. Jean Hollerith Case, a granddaughter of Lucia, remembers, "We were so fascinated as children that the greenhouse had big movable panels on the roof that opened and shut, and its own furnace." Drains in the terra-cotta floor and indoor hoses were unique additions to a private greenhouse of that time.

Another granddaughter, Lucia Beverly Hollerith Lefferts, recalls going through the greenhouse as a tiny girl on her way to play in the garden. "I remembered being wowed by the wonderful fragrance of the nasturtium that was climbing up the wall, especially because it was so warm and moist in there. And there was a vibrant pink bougainvillea, and a huge strange-looking staghorn fern on the wall, and lots of daffodils and hyacinths. We would eat dinner in the dining room and look through the French doors, and there were always plants everywhere."

After Lucia Beverly died, her three unmarried daughters took over caring for garden and greenhouse, which hosted garden tours and the Georgetown Garden Club meetings. "I remember my aunt was so proud of the strawberry sandwiches that she served, and all the ladies thought they were so delicious. I couldn't believe it because I'd never heard of a strawberry sandwich," Lucia recalls, laughing.

Sally Hollerith Nietsch, another granddaughter, remembering the blue ribbons her aunts won at the garden shows, is grateful for having inherited their passion for gardening: "They gardened until their last breaths, and it gave them such great pleasure. Some of the plants from the greenhouse I have in my own home now, and it is a nice memory."

In 1994 the last of Herman and Lucia's children died, at ninety-four years old. Two years later the home, which had become an historical landmark in Georgetown, was sold to its second owners, interior designers Rob Brown and Todd Davis. "We responded to many things about this home. It was very well built, had beautiful high ceilings and lovely big rooms, but we especially loved the greenhouse and the extraordinary garden," says Rob.

"I just thought it would be so incredible to have a greenhouse; it's an ultimate luxury in a home," says Todd. The two immediately began collecting plants and nurturing them in the greenhouse. "I have English parents—the English are known for their green thumbs, and I've definitely inherited some of that. I knew it could be a fun and unique hobby, so we really wanted to give it a shot," says Rob. Conferring with Hollerith family members about the plants that did best, they planted nasturtium and began filling the wooden benches with rare orchids and other unusual plants.

"Initially it went really well. We had lots of plants and enjoyed the terrific sense of green and humidity, especially during the Washington winters, which can be so drab and dreary," remembers Rob. Eventually however, the pressures of work and the expense of running a greenhouse forced them to reconsider its use. "It became very time-consuming, taking all our hours after work and on the weekends, and there were major heating bills. Without the time to really put into it, we found our biggest crop was beginning to be bugs," he jokes.

Todd also felt they were not getting much use out of the lovely light-filled space. "We really found that we weren't using the greenhouse as much as we'd have liked. There were built-in benches, so it wasn't designed for furniture; it was a real working greenhouse. We were not really able to sit and enjoy being in there, and we just began to think that maybe we should modernize it."

The room was converted from a working greenhouse to a comfortable formal conservatory designed for entertaining, dining, and relaxing. Terra-cotta floors were changed to limestone and marble, and the drains were closed off. The glass ceiling was painted white to modulate the intense,

sometimes searing sunlight, and the once-magical ventilation panels were closed to accommodate the air-conditioning. A nineteenth-century Venetian chandelier found in the pair's travels replaced the original lights, and antiques and comfortable upholstered sofas and chairs took the place of the old wooden benches and plant stands. Eight-foot palms, towering tree ferns, orchids, and blooming hibiscus landscaped the room instead of seedlings in flats, struggling cuttings, and bags of potting soil.

The frosted glass above the exterior door was changed to clear glass to afford a view of majestic tree canopies and the acre of garden, which runs the length of the city block. "Since we moved here, we have been working to restore this magnificent garden, and we realized that until we redid the greenhouse we really didn't have a place to sit and view it from the house. When you are in the greenhouse, you really feel you are outside, yet you are protected from the hot sun or the cold," says Todd.

Viewed from the greenhouse, the garden flows almost seamlessly from indoors to out. Grand trees and shrubs, the foundation of Lucia's original design, give structure to today's garden as well. "Once we got out there and began to really go through things, we found there were some very prized specimens there," says Todd.

The centerpiece is a majestic hundred-year-old cedrela tree, bordered by a sea of meticulously manicured lawn. A thirty-foot limb, gnarled with time, extends horizontally a few feet above the ground, the outer branches gesturing graciously like a dancer's fingertips. Rob comments, "This is a wonderful old tree that has developed a very unusual shape. We think of it as a real living sculpture. It is great to sit in the greenhouse and look at it. In the summer it is beautiful because it's green with leaves, but in some ways it is even more beautiful in the winter, when it's bare and you can really see the architecture." There are also several styrax trees and a magnificent weeping cherry with cascades of pink in the spring. "People look at the cherry tree, and they are astonished because they didn't know they grew so large," says Todd.

Influenced by the gardens at the British Embassy, where they recently completed the interiors, and by the Rockefeller gardens in Maine designed by Beatrix Farrand, Brown and Davis restored the garden with great care. Areas around the trees were cleared and leveled by hand to protect the old roots, and a carpet of pristine lawn was put down. More than one hundred boxwoods supplied the essential framework to the formal English design, and a rose garden with dozens of varieties was planted. An

Facing page: Blush-pink peonies, fresh cut from the garden, are placed center stage in anticipation for Sunday brunch.

Since we moved here we have been working to restore this magnificent garden, and we realized we really didn't have a place from the house where we could sit and view it.

herbaceous garden with a scalloped, undulating border was laid out in full view of the greenhouse, with mock orange, lilac, daylilies, chrysanthemum, peonies, indigo, and crape myrtle; according to Rob, "The border creates movement and rhythm and color in the garden."

Special lighting was installed on the trees to create a soft moonlit ambience in the evening. "It's quite a sight from the greenhouse," says Todd. "One of our guests said recently that it is the most romantic place in all of Washington to have dinner."

Once the garden was completed, the greenhouse offered a front-row view of its ever-changing living portrait during all the seasons. "It is so nice during the winter when the sun brightens and heats up the room," says Todd. "We get a little moisture from the plants, so it becomes a bit humid like the summer, and you can look out at the snow and the outline of the cedrela. Sometimes it rains, and you get the patter on the roof. It's also nice to sit in here during the summer and enjoy the beautiful surroundings but still be protected from the elements."

A natural place for friends to gather, the greenhouse is frequently used for lunches, small dinner parties, or cocktails and appetizers before dinner in the formal dining room. "It's a great way to start a party. It is a very uplifting room and it really helps to elevate the spirits and get the party going," says Todd. "I love to bring friends in here for dinner," adds Rob. "It makes people feel very special to be in this room. We get a lot of gasps when people come in here."

Brown and Davis have managed to give themselves the very thing they strive to offer their clients. "I like to come in on Sunday mornings and lie on the sofa with a cup of coffee and read the newspaper, and I also come in here during the day for quiet reflection. It is our role in our business to create tranquillity and beauty for people, and I find that we've created that very thing for ourselves here," says Rob. "It's a very magical place."

Facing page: June 1996, when Brown and Davis first acquired the property they maintained the working greenhouse style of the original owners. The remodeled conservatory of today is far better suited to their lifestyle.
(Photo courtesy Brown and Davis)

Growing Ferns Indoors

FERNS HAVE BEEN AROUND FOR MORE THAN 300 MILLION YEARS and are among the oldest and most fascinating group of plants in the world. Their beauty and often easy care make them an immensely popular plant among indoor gardeners. Their leaves can be delicate and lacy or glossy and straplike; almost all make attractive foliage plants, given the right conditions. Unlike other plants, ferns do not produce flowers and seeds, but reproduce from spores. Fern lovers admire them not for the drama of blossoms but for their lovely, unique foliage.

Ferns can be attractive as tabletop plants, hanging in baskets, or as floor specimens. Boston ferns, among the most fashionable parlor ferns, can grow to a substantial size. Maidenhair ferns, with their delicate, airy emerald green fronds, are a wonderful plant for a humid space like the bathroom. The bird's-nest fern, named for its large clumps of bold, glossy green leaves, comes from the tropics and is very tolerant of home conditions. The staghorn fern, a handsome, curious plant that is sure to be an exotic addition to any collection, is a tree dweller in the wild; it can be mounted on bark and displayed on the wall, or placed in a hanging basket.

Ferns thrive in a humid environment in nature, so providing them with the extra humidity they require in our heated, air-conditioned homes is often the major challenge to indoor gardeners. Bathrooms or kitchens can make

Left: A Boston fern remains robustly healthy in the relative low light of this northern window.

Facing page: Many ferns are epiphytes and will do well hanging and with little soil as long as they receive adequate water and nutrients.

104

ideal homes for them, and ferns do well placed with other plants, since grouping tends to increase humidity. Some, such as Boston or staghorn ferns, need 50 to 70 percent humidity to do well. Hosing them down in the shower is a good way to give them extra moisture and also to keep them clean and pest-free. Placing the plant on a pebble tray with water and spraying with water once or twice a day will also help.

Ferns usually appreciate the low-light situations in our homes and prefer medium to bright indirect light. They also like temperatures similar to those we like. Most will do best in 65 to 75 degrees, though some don't mind dipping into the 50s. Boston and asparagus ferns can easily take temperatures as low as 40 degrees as well as warmer temperatures, which is helpful if one prefers to keep them on a balcony or porch.

Ferns like to be kept moist but not soggy; never allow them to sit in water. These plants are sensitive to fertilizer and should be fed in the warmer months of spring, summer, and early fall with a solution of all-purpose organic fertilizer diluted by half. Withhold fertilizer in the winter. Use a well-drained, richly organic potting soil.

For a list of additional ferns to grow indoors, see appendix B, p.153.

Grand and Formal:
Private
Conservatories

*P*rivate conservatories conjure up thoughts of the grand classical orangeries built for the nobility in Europe. Magnificent structures that housed hundreds of citrus trees to supply the winter table, they spanned hundreds of feet in the garden, with carved stone columns and elaborate marble floors, and doubled as elaborate crystal-palace ballrooms in the summertime.

The romantic appeal of these lovely old structures, many of which still exist today, dims in the harsh light of reality: they are prohibitively expensive to heat, their cast iron frames are prone to rust and their wood to rot, and their single-glazed windows are often leaky. Many of them remain unused even in the grandest European estates.

It is only in the last forty years that private conservatories have seen a dramatic revival of popularity. New advancements in technology such as the introduction of double-glazed windows and the development of new automated maintenance systems, coupled with the idea that a conservatory can also be a place to eat, relax, and entertain, have given them a new appeal for the modern family. The most common complaint I hear from new conservatory owners is that the rest of the house is often abandoned in favor of the conservatory's sunny comfort.

Previous spread: Giant palms loom overhead in this Connecticut conservatory, creating a natural canopy for the shade-lovers planted below.

Far left: This phalaenopsis is an easy-care orchid that will thrive in most homes.

Left: These tropical trees from left to right are a Tillandsia bromeliad, a banana tree and a Veitchia merrillii.

Greenwich Indoor Retreat

The sweet childhood memory of gardening with her mother in the loamy Wisconsin soil planted a seed with Sheree Friedman, which germinated during her years of career building and urban living in New York City.

In the late 1980s the Friedmans decided to leave New York. Sheree, an architect and painter, along with her husband, Jerry, founder and CEO of several companies specializing in mortgage insurance and financial guaranties, who retired in 1999, and their daughter, Sarah, were ready to exchange urban life for the serenity of a spacious suburban estate. Although they were not experienced gardeners, they both felt the need to learn, and to be surrounded by gardens and nature. Jerry began studying rare orchid cultivation, and Sheree was yearning to get back to her roots. "I grew up in the Midwest, so I've always been connected to nature," she says. "I found that our little daughter had rarely seen grass or touched foliage, and my husband had been enclosed in the canyons of Wall Street. I wanted us to be planting things, be closer to nature and get our fingernails dirty."

Facing page: The tropical room in this Connecticut conservatory provides a perfect environment for plants that appreciate a warm, humid climate.

Right: Sheree Friedman finds the serene environment of her conservatory conducive to solitude and meditation.

The answer came in a five-acre property they were shown in 1988 in Greenwich, Connecticut. With dozens of giant mature beech trees, weeping willows, a linden allée, massive, full-grown rhododendrons, and lawns sweeping to a tranquil lake, the property had the substance and maturity in which to build a paradise.

The Friedmans wanted their new house to be a visual gateway to the outside. "We literally wanted to be sitting in nature," says Sheree, who is a graduate of Pratt Institute's School of Architecture and a student of *feng shui.* "We wanted our home to have good energy and to integrate important principles like light and air flow, and to help us have joy when we're here. Doing that makes a wonderful feeling that comes through in your family relationships and your work and all your life."

Renowned architect and designer Warren Platner, a longtime professional and personal friend, was called in to collaborate with Sheree on the new contemporary home, the gardens, and a conservatory that would provide year-round contact with nature. Sheree's sketches were used for the final plans, which called for a complete renovation of the existing Asian contemporary home. Hallways, narrow spaces, and walls were eliminated to create an open, airy setting, and additional rooms were added to the already spacious home. Great expanses of twelve-foot-high floor-to-ceiling glass were installed to integrate the interior and exterior, to underscore views of the boundless landscape, and to reflect seasonal changes. The project took two years to complete.

"This house is very unusual because we designed it and the gardens around it to relate to each other, in one process. Each room in the house has been carefully planned to look out to terraces, fountains, gardens, pools and a lake," says Platner. "The conservatory is really one of the

The conservatory allows them to walk through a beautiful garden every day during every season of the year.

many gardens on the property, and because it is a tropical one, it is indoors."

The Friedmans wanted the airiness of the new design to be reflected in every part of the home. It was also vital that the experience of coming home would be pleasurable. Skylights illuminated utilitarian areas, and because the family generally arrives through the garage, the conservatory was planned as a transition from there to the main house.

On a cold, snowy Connecticut day the Friedmans come home to the warm, steamy fragrance of a tropical island, the soothing sound of trickling water from a hand-carved stone fountain, and a vibrant array of tropical palms, banana trees, orchids, ferns, and camellias. "The conservatory allows them to walk through a beautiful garden every day during every season of the year," says Platner.

When the conservatory was first planned, the Friedmans

thought they would use it as a working greenhouse to grow organic fruits and vegetables. As the project developed, however, their conception of it changed, and it became a traditional formal conservatory, landscaped with exotic tropical plants. In the style of some large estate or public conservatories, soil-rich flower beds were built directly into the floor, rather than using pots as do most private conservatories.

Platner researched conservatory plantings with the director at the New York Botanical Gardens Conservatory and at the Planting Fields Conservatory on Long Island. He specified the foundational plants for the conservatory with an eye to duplicating a tropical environment that would require 68- to 72-degree temperatures. A pair of stairs made of patterned teakwood was built to lead to a small observation balcony where visitors are invited to view the garden from high, and to appreciate the multilevel plantings.

"I suppose one of the most unusual things about this greenhouse is why it was built," says Jerry. "It represents a wonderful place in the winter where we can relax and feel good about being around green and pretty things, but this conservatory was built by artists and architects rather than gardeners. We understand beauty and color and light and space and come about it from that vantage. It's probably a little unorthodox compared to why most greenhouses are built, by people who understand flowers and plants." The Friedmans also consider the conservatory a laboratory: "We always intended that we would learn about the plants and their needs, and that has always been an important part of its purpose too."

Today giant *Veitchia merrillii* and banana trees that nearly reach the twenty-five-foot high glass ceiling create a canopy of trees in the junglelike room. Kentia palms and midlevel vines such as *Cissus striata* and *Petrea volubilis* 'Albiflora' add blossoms and unique interest to the collection of plants. A delightfully perfumed *Mitriostigma axillare* fills the room with sweet fragrance, and a *Burbidgea schizocheila* from the ginger family helps to complete the tropical feel. Baskets with Boston ferns, or a mixture of maidenhair and staghorn ferns, hang from the balcony. Tiny groundcovers, *Soleirolia soleirolii* and *Cyanotis kewensis,* creep along the floor of the garden, completing the several height levels that replicate a natural jungle landscape. To satisfy their original idea of growing organic fruits and vegetables, the Friedmans have also planted citrus trees. A specialty of Sheree's is her lime pie, made from the fruit of trees in the conservatory.

Rob Girard, a horticulturist and specialist in greenhouse plant design and maintenance, cares for the Friedman conservatory. "This is a very special place because of the extraordinary design and because it serves this family so well," he says. "It is unique because everything is grown directly in beds, and it is more like a true conservatory than others I see."

He and the Friedmans agreed from the beginning that the greenhouse would be maintained organically and that chemicals would not ever be used. "I wouldn't take a job where the owners wanted to use chemicals, and the Friedmans probably wouldn't have hired anyone who did, so it worked out well for all of us." Soap sprays and other organic measures are used successfully to control pests and diseases, and plans are under way to begin experimenting with beneficial insects to combat those that are destructive.

Above: Adjacent to the main conservatory, the cold room holds plants adapted to cooler, more temperate regions.

Facing page: This round window frames the ever-changing vista of the garden through all seasons.

Building a collection of more uncommon plants is foremost in the plan. "The thing that really excites me about my work are the plants, and I really love unusual and collectable plants," says Girard. "I am working with the family now to increase their collection of more unusual things. They are great to work with because they are so eager to learn and make this grow."

A smaller cold room, kept at 52 degrees, was built adjacent to the main conservatory for growing plants from cooler, more temperate regions, such as camellias and some orchids. A plumbed potting room was also added to facilitate transplanting and potting, and doubles as a feline hotel for the family's three cats, Casper, Misfit, and Spock.

A four-foot round window, placed center stage in the conservatory, provides views to the pool and one of the exterior perennial gardens. Encased in hand-molded brick, it connects the tropical interior to the seasonal exterior. Outside in winter, mounds of glistening winter snow and skeletal trees create an intriguing contrast to the lush and steamy inside; in autumn crisp golden leaves lie windblown from the trees. The spring brings a vibrant fusion of color from tulips and spring bulbs, and beds of perennials create a summertime riot, painting an ever-changing portrait of the seasons through the portal of this Connecticut glass house.

The fifty-five-foot-long brick-and-glass conservatory was designed to meld perfectly into the new home renovation and the materials chosen exemplify the owners and architect's perfectionism. Soft pink hand-molded brick specially made for the project frames the glass and gives a rosy hue to the conservatory. Unique thresholds, electrically operated glass panels, and state-of-the-art misting, heating, and ventilation systems were installed. Decorative cast iron floor grates and distinctive roof finials were included in the final design.

Paul Zec from Amdega Conservatories, who was brought in to provide the glass and metal components for the conservatory says, "Everything about this job was exceptional. The architects and owners wanted everything customized, and only the best quality. They like things a little different, and they like to push the envelope."

The Friedmans sometimes sit and enjoy a glass of wine in the conservatory. Seventeen-year-old Sarah grows herbs, and Jerry reads and tends, the plants. "I finds it relaxing to just cut back the leaves or spent blossoms. It's a beautiful place to be," he says.

"The conservatory has been more important to us than we imagined," says Sheree, who practices yoga and meditates there daily. "We enter our home through the mist and the foliage of banana and lime trees that are producing fruit, and the scent of camellias and orchids. And we carry this wonderful flow of positive environmental *ch'i* into the heart of our home. It's a great gift."

A fountain fills its surroundings with the serene music of nature.

Building a Garden under Glass

IF THE COLD DAYS OF WINTER FEEL AS IF THEY ARE GETTING LONGER, if the snowy sidewalks feel more slippery, if the rain seems to fall harder, if you yearn to get your hands in the soil and the sight of an early spring blossom is far more of a relief than it used to be, maybe it's time to replace winter with spring—and do it without moving to Florida.

Many homeowners find reprieve from the winter blues by installing conservatories in their homes. These, as well as providing homes for plants, have found use as family rooms, places to entertain and eat, or spots to relax and view the exterior garden, protected from the elements. They give growing families additional space, and make excellent pool houses or quiet work spaces.

The conservatory's most popular use, however, is to combine living space with an indoor landscape where one can grow everything from herbs and vegetables to exotic jungle plants and twenty-foot palm trees; where the air is fresher and more fragrant, and the winter is kept at bay.

There are, however, a few things to consider when adding a conservatory. It is essential to establish the purpose of the room and the way it will be used from the start. If it is intended as extended living space, make sure it is easily accessible from the rest of the house. Many conservatories go unused because they were placed in a part of the home that was not convenient. One also needs to consider the architectural integrity of your home. An architect can recommend a suitable site.

Architects often work with companies that manufacture the components for conservatories and offer prefabricated models. It is desirable to investigate these products before making a final decision about your conservatory, the manufacturers are knowledgeable, and have tested their designs. Reputable companies should be well informed about managing the sun and heat—which can become oppressive in glass buildings even on cool days—ventilation, watering systems, and drainage. Ask to see other private conservatories they have built, and speak with the owners about the quality and dependability of their service.

Many orchids need the cooler environment that the cold room provides. These orchids benefit from a state-of-the-art electrically operated automatic misting system.

Discuss with the company such matters as the benefits of building with an aluminum frame or a wooden frame, and glass versus plastic products. Wood is often thought to be a more attractive choice for homes with more classical or formal architectural designs, but it can be very difficult to maintain and tends to warp and shift with age. An alternative is to use a faux paint technique to make an aluminum frame appear woodlike.

Double-paned glass can be helpful with insulation, but if it is not adequately sealed, moisture can build up between the panes and cause the windows to fog. Be certain the company will guarantee against this happening, and replace the glass if it does.

Conservatories can range in price from a few thousand dollars to hundreds of thousands. Whether it is as elaborate and formal as grand Victorian with lacy ironwork, marble floors, automated irrigation, ventilation, and heating systems, or as humble as a cozy addition off the garage. It can serve as a link between the house and the garden, bring nature into the home, and provide a place to nurture your plants and your family all year round.

Montgomery Palm Court

A TWENTY-FOUR-YEAR-OLD ARMY AIR CORPS CADET with flaming red hair and fiery ambition to match, he sped along the familiar country road, flanked by golden knee-high summer grasses, and was mesmerized by the achingly beautiful southern countryside that stretched out before him. This landscape would capture the imagination of the young Winton "Red" Blount, and fuel an enduring dream: here on these yellow grass fields, he would build one of the grandest Georgian estates that Alabama had ever seen.

It was 1945, and Blount had just returned from the war. With a pocketful of borrowed money, he was on his way to purchase a few tractors, so he and his brother Houston could start a ditch-digging business that they would call Blount Brothers Construction. Four decades later Blount Brothers Construction was Blount International; it had built the Cape Canaveral launch pad, the New Orleans Superdome, and the $2 billion King Saud University.

Left: Winton and Carolyn Blount.

Facing page: This grand formal conservatory complements the Georgian architecture of the Blounts' home.

Left: A bird's-nest fern rests on a Corinthian capital.

Facing page: The garden entry into the conservatory is filled with a lush assortment of orchids and tropical plants.

Having accomplished his first objective, to develop one of the largest construction companies in the world, Winton had moved on to another goal—the estate of his boyhood dreams. He hired preeminent Georgian architect Mott Schmidt to design a home that would become a pristine example of the style. The grand redbrick mansion, named Wynfield, was situated in the heart of 140 acres in rural Montgomery, Alabama. With miles of landscaped gardens, stables, and pastures for sheep and horses, it would be used to entertain, but also make a comfortable home to raise five children. According to Winton, "The original concept was to have a beautiful, distinctive home. But we also wanted it to be livable, and for many years it has been just that."

In 1969 Blount accepted Richard Nixon's appointment as postmaster general of the United States, and served for four years. As the Blounts' lifestyle became more demanding, their home became an important spot for meetings and entertaining, as well as a retreat from a busy life. It became apparent that the formal dining room, which accommodated fourteen for dinner, would not suffice: "We needed a place where we could entertain and have dinners for large groups of people. I wanted to be able to seat my whole family in one room for the holidays, and we are more than thirty."

Concerned about compromising the architecture, however, Winton was reluctant to build onto the house or enlarge the formal dining room. A chance visit to a home with a grand conservatory during a trip to England provided a possible answer. Architect Bobby McAlpine and interior designer Ray Booth were hired to work together on the conservatory. "The Blounts were looking for entertaining space, but they wanted something with historical reference, something that would not destroy the original design of the home," says Booth. "They wanted to know what existed in history that could be used as a model, and they

> *"It is so vertical and regal and deeply glamorous that people are kind of shocked when they walk in there."*

talked to us about a conservatory, which of course was a perfect solution."

McAlpine took great pains with the conservatory's design: "It was my great horror that I would add something onto that lovely Georgian house that would look like I'd been there, and so every attempt was made to make it look as original as possible." The fifty-by-thirty-foot glass structure was built onto the southern side of the house. The entryway, a long, narrow foyer that was originally an open patio, connects the living room to the conservatory, an inviting antechamber that draws the visitor in. An antique fountain is stationed against the crimson brick wall. Ficus, holly, schefflera, dracaena, philodendron, and heaps of orchids and bromeliads are arranged in levels to create a massive, multihued tropical arrangement.

Entry into the conservatory, with its glistening chandeliers, twenty-five-foot ceilings, roof-high palm trees, and grand eighteenth-century fire front, is dramatic. "It is so vertical and regal and deeply glamorous that people are kind of shocked when they walk in there," says McAlpine.

Veitchia sp. palms in huge rusticated pots line the room, creating a second-story ceiling of green. Cycads and bird's-nest ferns in copper kettles and blooming orchids, chosen seasonally from the estate's greenhouse, fill the glass-enclosed space with color and fragrance. Retractable ceiling shades help to modulate the often-intense sun.

McAlpine had a clear vision of what he hoped to achieve: "This room is in the tradition of a great palm court. It would be a place where people would come and convene in a space that is beautifully and opulently furnished and have cocktails and visit under the palm trees, and this is their use as well."

Upholstered banquettes, small cocktail or dining tables, and chairs in soft fabrics add warmth to the room. "It definitely needed cozying up. With all that steel and glass, we felt we needed plants and as much fabric and acoustical

*The conservatory and the two gardens beyond it
are really like three gardens — one flows so
graciously into the next.*

attendance as possible," says McAlpine. Colors would also add warmth. "All the colors are variations of stone, and there isn't really any white-white. There is a little oyster and some pale gold. It was important that we have a color palette that wouldn't fade or distort. Red would have been pink in a year in that room."

Marrying the indoor space with the exterior gardens was crucial. Fourteen acres of landscape gardens recently renovated by New York landscape designer Edwina von Gal include a formal reflecting pool garden, a chapel garden, a wild border garden, an orchard with dozens of crape myrtles, roses, and a kitchen garden that supplies employees and a soup kitchen in town with fresh fruits and vegetables. All garden paths eventually lead to the conservatory.

Directly adjacent to the conservatory are the informal pool garden on the west and the more formal conservatory garden on the east. Doors lead out from the conservatory to each: "The conservatory and the two gardens beyond it are really like three gardens because one flows so graciously

into the next," says Ray Booth. "It just so happens that one of them is indoors." Bobby McAlpine explains it in his own way: "It was my hope that the conservatory would re-create the outdoors in a way. It is totally transparent, and it very much honors the garden on both faces, so in that way it has been very successful."

From a grand glass ballroom that accommodates 300 people at a formal supper to an intimate summertime dining place for a few friends, the conservatory has served the Blounts well. Here they can bring friends, fund-raise for the numerous charities they support, or enjoy an intimate breakfast or afternoon tea in a cozy, sunlit corner.

"This is a room that has great stature," says McAlpine. "It makes you hold your back straight. It's like when you walk the streets in Paris, you feel so tall and beautiful; I think it's a little like that when you walk into that room. It's the proportion of it with those palms, tall cast columns and draperies, and the importance and great dignity of the space. It just makes you think, 'Ain't life grand'."

Guests are ushered from the public rooms of the house into the conservatory through this tranquil foyer.

Designing with Plants

CREATE A MOOD, ENHANCE A ROOM'S FORMALITY or casual comfort, generate drama, or produce a gentle, calming environment. You can do it all with the right plant placement and decor. Decorating with plants adds life and finishes a room in a way few other accessories can.

Grouped plants can create a stunning visual effect; they also benefit from the additional humidity created when they are close together. Combining plants, as they grow in the wild, helps to create a natural, healthy microclimate. Arrange taller plants toward the back, and shorter in the front. Use inverted flowerpots, bricks, or a wooden crate to elevate plants in the back if necessary. The plants in front will hide these props, and the layers of plants will produce a pleasing composition.

Indoor plants are often chosen for the interest and beauty of their foliage rather than for their flowers, so look for plants with variegated, textured, or unusually shaped foliage. Cacti with bulbous appendages, caudiciforms with swollen trunks, ferns with airy floating leaves, or fan-shaped palms with dark green fronds can add unusual and creative accents.

Left: Boldly marked calatheas make a striking statement.

Facing page: Bromeliads, ferns, palms, and orchids thrive in a humid environment.

A single specimen plant can also make an important architectural statement. For example, large palms can be a focal point in a room, although plants do not have to be large to be given the spotlight. A pair of dracaenas with striped yellow-and-red leaves or a *Ficus benjamina* with a braided trunk can be an architectural eye-catcher.

Using lighting to enhance the effect of a single plant or a group can add drama. A light directed to the front of an *Anthurium crystallinum*, for example, will underscore its large heart-shaped leaves and highlight its glistening white veins. When backlit, the reddish leaves of a *Kohleria* 'Dark Velvet' will take on new life and glow dramatically. Sometimes it is interesting to create shadows that enhance the shape of plants. Some palms and large cacti, for example, will throw magical shapes against a white wall when lit properly. Experiment—move your plants and lights around to get the most from lighting.

Plants can be chosen to create an ambience that will complement your room design. Citrus might evoke a sunny Mediterranean countryside, bamboos remind one of the Far East, orchids make us think of dense tropical rain forests, and howea palms recall turn-of-the-century ballrooms.

Remember that decorating with plants is art in progress. Don't be timid: try new effects, move things around, and experiment. Above all, have fun.

CHAPTER
SIX

*Living with
Profusion*

A well-appointed room would be incomplete without plants to add the finishing touch; they add the spark that gives energy and vitality to everything else. The environments in individual rooms in a home can differ significantly, however, and a wise indoor gardener will consider conditions in each room before bringing a new plant home. A kitchen, for instance, often has fluctuating temperatures near the stove, refrigerator, or freezer. A well-traveled room in most homes, it can be subject to sudden drafts. All these things can upset even the most robust plants, but it is an ideal site for herbs, which are usually tolerant of these conditions. Bathrooms are warm, humid, and often don't have lots of light; they are a good home for ferns and some orchids. Hallways are sometimes darker than the rest of the house, and can be drafty, with doors opening and shutting. Tough, shade-loving plants like *Aspidistra elatior* or *Monstera deliciosa* will do well here. Succulents like drier conditions and will be happy in a home with forced-air heating, which dries the air.

Plants can have various decorative functions in the rooms in our homes. A cactus speaks of a casual, southwestern feel, and palms might recollect the grand formality of the Victorian era. Orchids convey elegance, and herbs and vegetables in the kitchen suggest comforting foods and a safe, warm place that is the family's emotional hearth.

Previous spread: A lion's-head fountain makes for a surprising addition to a New York City dining room.

Facing page: Colonies of plants, including birds-of-paradise, dracaenas with shiny, stiff leaves, several varieties of calathea, alacacias, chartreuse selaginella, and orchids combine to dramatic effect in this small rain forest garden.

Right: A water feature in an indoor garden can add drama and substance.

Soho Urban Jungle

THE SUNLIT ITALIAN LOGGIA HAD THE PATINA of ancient walls, overhung by lush foliage. The fragrance of fresh, earthy vegetation permeated the air, and a gentle symphony of water dribbled from a stone fountain. The spot was dreamy and reminiscent of lazy sun-drenched holidays.

It took a tiny shake into reality to remind me that we were in an old factory in the concrete center of New York City on a damp, gray winter day. The first time I saw the indoor dining room of Scott Appell and Bill Shank's SoHo loft, I thought I'd seen a mirage.

When Scott moved into the loft six years ago, he brought his collection of houseplants and many grand ideas. "I could see grape ivy growing up the posts and arbors with blossoms. I bought giant banana trees, blooming hibiscus, and citrus with fruit." As director of education for the New York Horticulture Society and author of five books about indoor and outdoor gardening, he encourages his students and readers to be individualistic, imaginative gardeners. He suggests they become educated

Left: Scott Appell with his cat Castor.

Facing page: The dining room teems with life, a sanctuary in the heart of New York City.

Three whimsical terrariums are tiny gardens in themselves.

about plants while being innovative and courageous. This philosophy is evident in his flora- and foliage-filled home.

The New York neighborhood where Scott gardens is accustomed to maverick residents. SoHo, once an industrial district, became famous in the 1960s as an enclave for artists, who lived illegally but cheaply in its large warehouse spaces.

P & G Lorillard constructed the building in 1876 as a chewing-tobacco-processing factory. Later it became a doll factory, and finally a storage facility for used corrugated boxes. In the early 1960s Bill purchased the old building with three others and immediately set out to make it a legal space for living. In the early 1970s the city granted permits to those with legitimate artist certification to convert the former SoHo factories into legal living lofts.

By 1973 the Feldman Brothers Used Corrugate Boxes Building had been divided into five legal living lofts, becoming the second legal loft building in SoHo. Bill's 4,000-square-foot full-floor loft had one electrical outlet, four dangling lightbulbs, bricked-over windows, and no plumbing.

Thirty years later, the loft boasts a state-of-the-art kitchen, contemporary bathrooms, formal brass lighting fixtures, and fashionable contemporary flooring. Its past is witnessed by twenty-foot-high tin-embossed ceilings and weathered brick walls. But nothing could be less reflective of its unique industrial beginning than the dining room's indoor jungle.

Scott's original fanciful ideas of light-loving tropicals and fruit-bearing trees didn't all work out. Nevertheless, the abundance of healthy plants and the unique interior landscape design have resulted in a comfortable get-away garden room, the product of many months of experimentation, a few failures, but no disappointments.

With energy bills soaring, the plant lights needed to grow things like hibiscus and fruit trees became too costly. The decision was made to replace the plants with selections requiring less light. The artificial lights were adjusted, and mirrors were hung to help increase and reflect existing light. "I tell people it is better to grow healthy, good plants that are for low light than mediocre ones for higher light. You can do anything with interior plants as long as you have enough light," Scott insists, "but at some point you must become practical and responsible about it."

Today a green canopy of a thick-trunked rubber plant (*Ficus elastica*), elephant ear (*Philodendron selloum*), and fiddle-leaf fig (*Ficus lyrata*), planted in della Robbia–style fiberglass pots, looms overhead. Dripping ferns, spiky palms, and exotic orchids add to the wondrous green jumble.

A gurgling stone waterfall built along a western wall bubbles into a pond with Shubunkin goldfish nipping at the water. Large rocks glisten with spreading mosses. Floating aquatic salvinia, a native of Brazil, ripples on the water's surface, and a blue channel catfish thrashes about. Flamingo flower (*Anthurium scherzeranum*), African mask plant (*Alocasia* sp.), and Chinese evergreen (*Aglanema modestum*) are tucked into and around the indoor waterfall and pond.

Three whimsical terrariums are tiny gardens in themselves. An Asian-style bonsai container planted with minuscule tropicals like fittonia, ferns, and silver-leafed syngonium has an antique lead Buddha figurine sitting center stage. Another is planted with miniature bamboo, carissa, bromeliads, and other baby-sized tropicals. Earthenware pots planted with ferns and dracaenas, also known as lucky bamboo, are accessorized with a museum replica of a Chinese garden ornament. A small glass square is planted with malpighia and tiny elms. The containers, made by Bill with cut glass and silicone aquarium sealant, are placed with care around the loft, like miniature parks.

A four-foot glass rosewood case made in Mexico as a shrine for church statuary was languishing in a damp basement when Scott spotted it several years ago. "I was so thrilled when I saw it, and I immediately knew just what I'd do with it." Cleaned and repaired, the case was fitted with a small fan, special lights, and a mirror to reflect light, and lined with glass and a sealant to protect against moisture. It was then planted with tiny phalaenopsis orchids and a

Facing page, left to right: Three terrariums. A museum replica of a Chinese garden ornament stands guard among earthenware pots planted with "lucky bamboo," a type of dracaena, and ferns; a decorative gravel mound supports plantings of malpighia and miniature elms; small phalaenopsis orchids, tillandsias, and ferns thrive in a Wardian case.

Above: The striking rosy hues of this bromeliad's foliage make it attractive even when it is not in bloom.

selection of species tillandsia and ferns. The glass-encased piece, called a Wardian case, is actually a terrarium that has been fitted into fine cabinetry. (See the sidebar "Making Terrariums and Wardian Cases," p.94.)

The original floors, built to accommodate heavy machinery, help support the heavy plants and damp soil, which would overburden a less sturdy structure. Some changes did have to be made in the loft, however. A special commercial drain and a watering system were installed in one of the bathrooms, where heavy-duty hooks support plants brought in for watering and draining.

Although Scott's expertise is apparent in the care he gives his plants and their health, he insists that anyone can enjoy this hobby. "It's not that this collection is so rare or unusual, but the plants are very healthy and large in size. This is the kind of gardening most people could do in their homes. It's healthy to be connected to nature, especially if you live in the city, but you should be willing to experiment and learn along the way."

Bill, a garden editor, founder of the Horticultural Alliance of the Hamptons, and a former commercial designer, took a special interest in creating the old-world environment. Antiques, lion-head fountains, and faux stone walls transport the visitor to another world. On one wall, the sepia-colored plaster seems to have broken away to reveal an ancient brick wall and a treasured artifact, an effect that took Bill little time to achieve. Another wall is fitted with old wrought-iron gates from the Astor estate in Long Island, perhaps placed as a subliminal tease to suggest there may be more grand gardens beyond.

"I lived in Italy, and I always fantasized about having an Italian loggia, and now I have one right in the middle of New York City," said Bill. The effect was enhanced using some inventive techniques. Cutouts from magazines and books on ancient history, enlarged on color copy machines designed for large-scale architectural drawings, were used as wallpaper. Special painting techniques add texture and age, their effect amazingly realistic in this Pompeiian room complete with Corinthian columns and decorative arches. "I suppose I could buy four-thousand-dollar wallpaper, but I'd rather spend ten dollars on color copies," Bill admits, laughing.

A narrow eighteenth-century French refectory table can be enlarged to seat up to twenty for dinner, but is used daily for meals or just a cup of tea or glass of wine. "When people come over, they always go right to this room, and they are usually pretty taken back when they see it. We rarely use the living room now. After all, most people don't get to sit under a tree when they have dinner in New York City," says Bill.

The result is a small paradise in the middle of one of the world's busiest cities, an oasis that speaks to the unique hopes of its occupants; each perceives the same beauty, and yet clearly enjoys it from the perspective of their own personal dreamlands. Says Bill, "This is really a fantasy for me. During the nice season we leave the windows open, and the warm breeze blows through. It reminds me of when I lived in Italy. But I love New York too, so I guess this space is the best of both worlds."

Says Scott, "I'd feel there was something missing in my life if I didn't do this. It is really necessary to fill the integral need I have as a human to garden and to nurture. But even if I did have an outdoor garden, I'd still do it anyway. Basically, I guess I just want to live in a jungle."

Made from a rosewood Mexican church shrine, this imposing Wardian case has been fitted to accommodate tropical plants.

137

Creating Light Where It Isn't

YOU CAN LIVE AT THE BOTTOM OF A CITY SKYSCRAPER or in a subterranean basement, have only north-facing windows looking out on a brick wall, or dwell in the middle of a dense, shadowed forest—and still grow a lush and inviting indoor garden. It just takes light.

A plant's metabolism is entirely dependent on light, and it will let you know when it's lacking. Spindly, leggy growth with lots of space between the nodes indicates insufficiency—the plant is trying to stretch toward the sun. Too much light, though, and foliage becomes bleached and scorched.

Lack of good light is probably the greatest limiting factor for growing plants indoors. If your home has large, unobstructed south- or west-facing windows, chances are that you can grow a variety of indoor plants. If not, supplemental lights can increase interior light.

To decide which artificial lights are best for your situation, it is good to understand a little about what the sun provides to encourage plant growth. The sun emits lights in all colors of the spectrum, but the blue ranges are most important for healthy foliage, bushiness, and to avoid spindly growth. Flowering plants need red-orange light to bloom and produce fruit.

Incandescent bulbs used in most domestic lights emit a high proportion of red rays, which are needed for flowering plants, but the total output of blue rays is insufficient, and so they are not suitable as a source for growing plants.

Artificial lights designed especially for growing plants indoors have become progressively more sophisticated in the last years. High-intensity discharge (HID) lamps and fluorescent lights boost the light available to plants, dramatically increasing plant growth. The brightest lights available and the best for growing larger plants are HID lamps, which can be installed anywhere in your home. They provide remarkable amounts of light and can be used as a substitute sun in isolated rooms or as a supplementary light source, providing longer or stronger hours of light each day.

Metal halide bulbs, a type of HID, emit light that is the strongest at the blue end of the spectrum and looks most like natural sunlight. They produce compact, leafy growth and is the best choice for an indoor garden in your home, since it does not distort the color of plants or people. Another type of HID, high-pressure sodium bulbs, emit

This tiny landscape under glass can thrive with artificial light.

138

a light concentrated in the red-orange spectrum, and thus promote flowering and fruiting. Be forewarned, however, that they distort the colors of everything they illuminate. This makes them less desirable in the home, unless they are on a timer set for a period when no one is at home or awake.

Fluorescent lights are ideal for seedlings and low-light plants, but are generally not considered as effective as HID. They have their benefits, however, new improvements, affordability, and lighting that is more pleasant for the home make them a popular option. Full-spectrum fluorescent bulbs are an alternative with a more natural light for the home, and they promote healthy plant growth.

San Francisco Jewel Box

A GIANT PALM CANOPY LOOMS LIKE A PROTECTIVE UMBRELLA over the moist, dripping rain forest. Birds-of-paradise glisten with bold, shiny foliage, damp moss creeps along the jungle floor, and the air is permeated with the sweet fragrance of orchids and mother earth.

The atmosphere awakens the senses, and one waits expectantly to hear the squawking of exotic parrots, leaves rustling underfoot from a slithering neighbor, or a naughty, screeching chimpanzee. But the latter scenario is unlikely, since this spot is actually an indoor tropical garden ingeniously created from a former light well in an elegant San Francisco mansion.

This California couple looked for many years for a home in San Francisco before they were shown the stately Georgian corner house in the mid-1980s. "We saw a lot of homes, but the minute I saw this one, I knew it was right," says the wife. Built in 1915, the 6,000-square-foot home had large gracious rooms and beautiful architectural detailing and paneling, but was not an overwhelming residence

Left: Landscape designer Davis Dalbok.

Facing page: This Chinese cane palm is the crowning glory of this small tropical garden.

Above: Mimicking their natural rain forest habitat, plants with low light needs are planted near the ground.

Below: Several varieties of calathea *are grouped to show off their opulent foliage.*

Facing page: Orchids glow like gems against white walls in this San Francisco garden.

for two. "We didn't need lots of bedrooms, and most beautiful older homes here were designed for big families. This one was ideal."

They began a year-long renovation. "There were so many things about the house that we loved, but the one thing that really bothered us was that it tended to be dark." Although rooms were large with high ceilings, light was subdued by the dark wood paneling and the fact that some of the rooms, like the study and kitchen, either had few windows or none at all.

"We just felt that we wanted to increase air flow and light," says the wife. Some of the walls around a small interior light well that ran through the center core of the building were removed, exposing the kitchen, interior backstairs, and study to the new open space. An electrically operated retractable glass ceiling was fitted at the top of the forty-foot light well to protect against the elements.

A flood of light and fresh air poured in—but the light also revealed ugly walls, dusty gravel, and exposed pipes of the light well. "It seemed odd to me that a home that had so much attention to details in other ways was built that way, but I guess they thought it would never be visible," she says . "Once they tore it all out, I thought, Oh, my gosh. What now? I had no idea what we might do with it. It was my husband's idea to put in a garden. That thought hadn't even occurred to me, since when I think garden, I think ground level, and this was a story above the ground."

Pipes were moved, walls were painted white to reflect more light, and the floor of the former light well was fitted with a waterproof metal pan and special drains. The area was planted, using common Mediterranean plants, by the designer who landscaped the exterior of the house.

In 2001 the couple decided that the garden needed to be renovated. "It was getting tired and needed to be redone. I had always thought that it had gone in slightly the wrong direction and should have been more tropical in feeling, so this was the opportunity to do it."

Davis Dalbok, a longtime acquaintance and respected San Francisco garden designer, came to view the site, and was inspired: "When I went to look, I was bowled over by how beautiful the home was, their incredible art collection and this wonderful little garden. There are some very beautiful old paintings in the study of exotic jungle scenes, with tropical foliage and Polynesian women. They've used opulent burgundy fabric and lots of rich tones in the furnishings. It reminded me of the rich tapestry of a jungle scene,

The atrium would become an important part of this wonderful home and relate to the art and interior design in a really strong way.

and I got very excited. I thought it was an opportunity to have the atrium become an important part of this wonderful home and relate to the art and interior design in a really strong way."

A fourteen-foot specimen *Rhapis excelsa,* lady palm, with an unusually beautiful curved cane was imported from Hawaii. "The palm is the crowning piece, and then we just sort of worked our way down with other foliage plants. I wanted it to be like a rain forest, with the palm as the canopy and the other plants as the understory," says Davis. *Dracaena compacta,* with stout, stiff leaves that resemble a pineapple plant, are massed in one corner and filter down through the garden. "This plant has always reminded me of those beautiful old botanical prints, so we used quite a few of them."

Davis appreciates the effect of using plants in mass: "We use colonies of plants rather than one here and one there because it is more effective." One thing he used extensively in groupings was calatheas. With their opulently colored foliage of hot pink stripes or multitoned greens, they add to the dramatic effect. A giant silver-green elephant's-ear, *Alocasia* 'African Mask,' is a rare variety from Florida, "such an unusual plant because of its extraordinary size and it just adds a real punch to the composition." In the foreground chartreuse *selaginella,* which resembles forest moss, and airy maidenhair ferns *(Adiantum pedatum)* are arranged around subtle groupings of rocks. "You can't go wrong using maidenhair fern in a garden. It's so lush, and just makes you feel so good. It's like eating a fresh salad," says Davis.

Although the garden looks as if it has been planted into beds of rich humus, plants are actually in containers, arranged on a metal waterproof membrane covered with a layer of gravel. Each pot is fitted with an emitter for the automatic watering drip system. Smaller plants are placed in front of larger, and huge sheets of moss are laid like a carpet to hide all pots and the watering equipment. "Davis is a master when it comes to making this garden look authentic," says the owner.

Spaces in the garden are left open for the owner's extensive collection of orchids when they are in bloom. "They have one of the most incredible collections of orchids, and most are very large and haven't been divided. They are a spectacular addition to the garden, but the design is such that it will stand alone without the orchids," says Davis. A four-foot purple *Vanda* hybrid from Thailand is tucked into the garden and will be enjoyed for weeks before it is replaced.

The microclimate created by the natural humidity of San Francisco, which with the ocean evaporation and cool natural fog ranges between 75 and 90 percent, the warmth of the home, and the retractable ventilating roof create an ideal tropical environment for plants. "It is really like a big terrarium," says Davis, "perfect for creating this jungle environment."

Easily seen from both the study and the back stairs, the garden is viewed and enjoyed often. "I suppose I see the garden most frequently going up and down the stairs during the day. It is delightful because I see different things going up than I do going down. The light changes so it's different scenery all the time and it just makes you feel so good," says the owner. "The study is always the room I go to if I want to relax or read, and if we are having another couple in for cocktails we go in there because it is a cozy, comfortable space, and the garden makes it very special. My favorite part is the surprise element. People just can't believe it."

"The garden is a little jewel," says Davis. "In the house there are many wonderful, glamorous rooms. But if I lived there, I would want to have my morning coffee in the study and smell the orchids. I'd look at the atrium and roll the roof back on a rainy day and pretend I was in Tahiti. What a great way to start the day," he adds with a smile.

A tiny tropical rain forest brings light
and fresh air into the library.

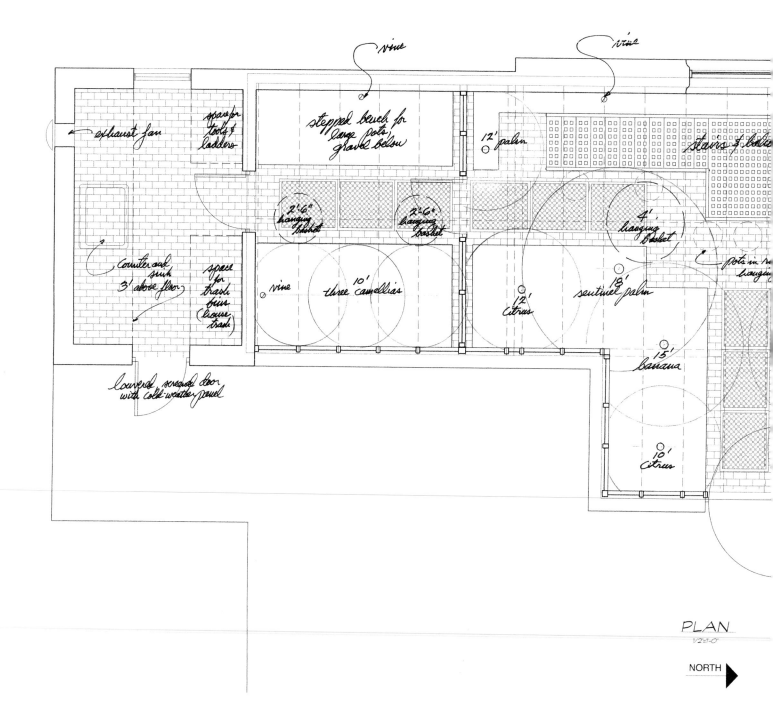

Perennial border garden and pool

exhaust fan

space for tools & ladders

stepped bench for large pots, gravel below

12' palm

stairs & balco[...]

Counter and sink 3' above floor

space for trash bins (house trash)

2'-6" hanging basket

2'-6" hanging basket

4' hanging basket

pots in t[...] hanging[...]

vine

three 10' camellias

12' Citrus

18' sentinel palm

louvered screened door with cold-weather panel

15' banana

10' Citrus

vine

vine

PLAN
1/2"=1'-0"

NORTH ▶

motor court

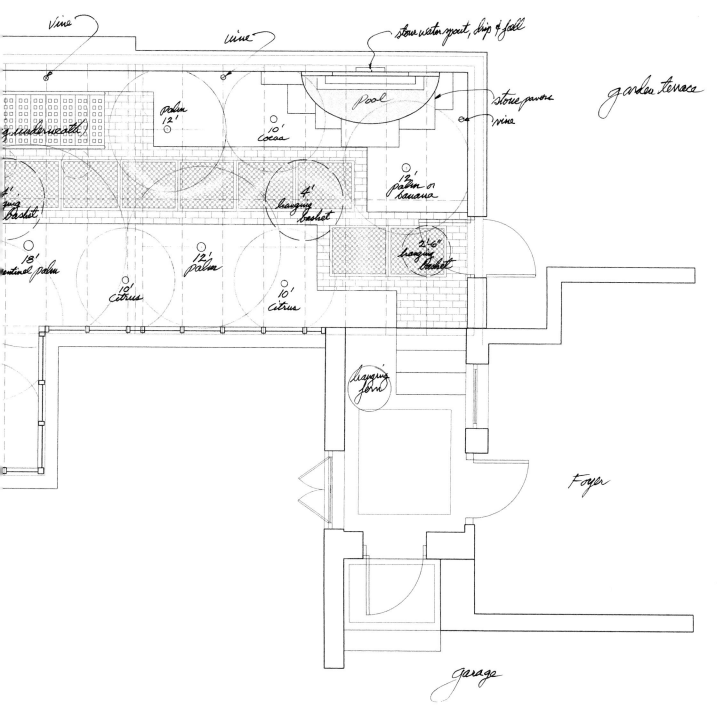

vine

vine

stone water spout, drip & fall

garden terrace

Pool

palm
12'

10'
cocoa

stone pavers

vine

4'
hanging
basket

12'
palm or
banana

g. underneath

4'
hanging
basket

18'
sentinel palm

12'
palm

2'-6"
hanging
basket

10'
citrus

10'
citrus

hanging
fern

Foyer

garage

THIS DETAILED BLUEPRINT DESCRIBES THE
ORIGINAL PLANTING SCHEME DESIGNED FOR
THE FRIEDMANS BY WARREN PLATNER
ASSOCIATES ARCHITECTS.

7/1/98

APPENDIX A
CARING FOR YOUR INDOOR PLANTS

LIGHT

Plants use light to manufacture fuel; regardless of how much care we give them in other ways, without enough light they will starve. Choosing the perfect spot for a plant with the right amount of natural sunlight* will ensure lush growth and abundant flowering, and accessing the light in your home before bringing in houseplants will help to guarantee success.

As a rule, south-facing windows bask in the most light and are good for sun worshipers like hibiscus, herbs, mandevillas, pelargoniums, cacti, passionflowers, nasturtium, and many more. If a plant is not producing blooms, or if growth is long and leggy with too much space between the nodes, it's likely there isn't enough light. Remember, however, that if plants that usually require high light have been kept long in shade, such as in a dark corner in the nursery, they will need to be reintroduced to the sunny position gradually to avoid burning. This can be done by pulling the plant back a few feet from the window at the first sign of white burn marks on the leaves, and slowing returning it to the sunny spot over a period of two weeks.

Windows that face east receive a half-day of morning sun, and western exposures have a half-day of afternoon sun. Begonias, gloxinias, camellias, mint, jasmine, and orchids generally do well in eastern or western light. In winter, it may be possible to introduce these lower-light lovers to a southern window; by the same token, in the summertime they may have to be protected even from an eastern or western exposure. If leaves curl, fade, or appear scorched, or if growth seems to stop, the likely culprit is too much light.

North-facing windows generally receive the least light, but even if this is your only option, you can still grow many beautiful houseplants. You may not have the bounty of blossoms that a south-facing window will bring, but there is a huge array of spectacular plants with showstopping foliage colors and leaf patterns. Ferns, aspidistras, dieffenbachia, dracaena, sansevieria, ivy, and philodendron are all wonderful, easy-care selections. Choosing attractive containers and grouping plants in layered displays with creative interplays of leaf textures and colors can help to dramatize a low-light situation.

Outside factors can change a lighting situation, so analyzing each position is important. A south-facing window, for instance, could be blocked by a large shade tree, stark white walls on the exterior of the building might intensify light, and a towering penthouse would have more light overall than lower floors.

To evaluate the light level in a specific location, try the paper test. Place a piece of white paper and position it near the foliage. Hold your hand above the paper and look at the shadow your hand casts. A shadow with sharp edges indicates bright light; a hazier shadow designates medium light; and a faint or absent shadow means low light. The test will give more accurate results if done during the brightest time of the day, which is generally between 10:00 A.M. and 2:00 P.M.

*See "Creating Light Where It Isn't," p. 138.

TEMPERATURE

Most houseplants are comfortable in the same conditions we like in our homes, so if our thermostats are set to 65–72 degrees Fahrenheit, we can be assured that our plants will be happy too. Many also prefer a slightly cool resting period at night, so will appreciate the energy-saving tactic of lowering the temperature 10–20 degrees at night.

Some plants, like begonias, bougainvilleas, and some African violets, prefer temperatures that never fall below 65 degrees. If it gets colder, they may become fooled into thinking winter has arrived, go into dormancy and drop their leaves.

On the other hand, some plants, such as winter-blooming jasmine, camellias, and acacias, won't bloom unless they are given a period at 50 degrees or cooler. If these winter-blooming plants fail to set buds, it may be because the room is too warm and they need to be moved to a cooler environment.

HUMIDITY

Many of our houseplants come from the rain forests or tropical areas of the world and are accustomed to an abundance of moisture in the air. Forced-air heating systems and air conditioners can cause the air to become dry, which is problematic for many houseplants.

Plants will react quickly to low atmospheric humidity. The first symptom is yellowing leaves or browning edges, followed eventually by a dramatic leaf drop. Humidity can be raised by adding a humidifier, placing a pan of water on a radiator or wood stove, or using a moisture tray. Put one inch of pebbles in a tray and fill with water to a level slightly below the top of the pebbles; refill as needed. The evaporating water will help to moisten the air.

Another solution for very dry environments is to choose plants that require low humidity. These include desert plants, like cactus, and many succulents.

WATERING

Overwatering is probably one of the most common causes of plant mortality, especially in winter when there is little else to occupy a gardener's attention. Most houseplants prefer to dry out between watering. Roots of plants that are kept constantly wet actually suffocate, so it is always better to underwater than overwater.

Watering on a set schedule seems to be the least effective method; it works better to respond according to the weather and season. Plants need more water in the summer when it is warmer, and also in the winter, when we crank up the thermostat and the air becomes warmer and drier.

As you get acquainted with your plants, you will learn how to judge when they need water. Poke your finger an inch into the soil to determine moisture, or pick up the plant to gauge the weight of wet versus dry soil. A plant that needs to be repotted will usually require more frequent watering. Conversely, a plant that is in a container too large for its size will often stay too wet for too long, a good reason for moving up only one container size at each repotting.

Many gardeners assume that wilting is a sure sign of a plant that needs watering, but in fact it can mean that the plant has been overwatered or has diseased or insect-infested roots, in which case additional watering will only make matters worse. Always check before watering.

Plants should be placed in the sink to be watered and allowed to drain entirely. Take care that larger plants, which cannot be moved, do not sit in a saucer of water.

PESTS AND DISEASES

Healthy plants are the best defense against insects and diseases. By maintaining a clean environment, removing debris like spent leaves and flowers immediately, and providing good air circulation, you can help to combat these nuisances. Segregate diseased plants immediately to avoid spreading infections, and scrutinize new plants before purchasing. Be assured, however, that even the best-maintained houseplants and the most careful gardeners can have problems.

The most common culprits are mealybugs, aphids, red spider mites, and whitefly, which can usually be controlled without chemicals. I highly recommend against using toxic materials in the home. For a plant infected with aphids, spraying with a solution of one teaspoon nondetergent dishwashing liquid mixed with a gallon of water will usually do the trick. Spray twice a day until insects have disappeared. Hanging yellow sticky traps or applying Naturalis O will combat whitefly. Red spider mites thrive in dry conditions and will usually disappear if the plant is sprayed or misted with cold water. Mealybugs can be removed with rubbing alcohol on a cotton swab.

FERTILIZING

Potted plants need nutrients, especially during the growing months from March through November. During the winter months when light levels are lower, extra nourishment is generally not needed; in fact, too much fertilizer can be unhealthy for a plant that is in a resting period.

Plants should be fed every two to three weeks with a weak solution of fertilizer. Never apply plant food in a more concentrated dose than that recommended on the label, or you will burn the plant. I generally start with a weaker solution, and work up to the recommended solution. A well-balanced organic fertilizer is best. The three numbers on the label indicate nitrogen, phosphorus, and potassium: a fertilizer labeled 10-10-10, for example, will supply equal parts of each and encourage healthy overall growth.

GROWING BULBS INDOORS

Louis XIV had the gilded halls of Versailles lined with fragrant, blooming hyacinths to help freshen the air in a court that relied more on cologne than soap. Although we may not be trying to cover up what a good bath might have done for Louis and company, we would nonetheless appreciate the delightful scents and stunning beauty of blooming indoor bulbs.

The technique of artificially supplementing the requirements of bulbs to bring them into flower outside their natural season is called forcing, and is a satisfying and fun process that can help you fashion a vibrant patch of garden in your living room.

Some of the easiest bulbs to force are those that don't require simulating a cold winter environment. Amaryllis come from tropical regions, paperwhites are semi-hardy members of the narcissus family, and both are easy to make grow in pots indoors. Amaryllis have vibrant, dramatic upright blossoms and paperwhites have intensely fragrant, white daffodil-like flowers.

Hardy bulbs, on the other hand, need weeks of cold temperatures in a chilling phase that duplicates their native winter, and then a warm home to fool the bulbs into believing spring has arrived, before they will bloom. Some bulbs can be purchased already pre-chilled, or they can be placed in the vegetable bin of your refrigerator to recreate the winter. Tulips, daffodils, hyacinths and crocus are good hardy candidates for indoor forcing.

Plant bulbs in a well-draining potting soil in a pot that is slightly larger than the bulb or bulbs you are planting. A single amaryllis, for example can be planted alone and be attractive. Five tulip bulbs will effectively fill a six-inch pot. You can also do a double layer planting by partially filling a deep container with soil, putting in a layer of bulbs, placing another shallow layer of soil and then finishing with a final layer of bulbs. Double layering allows you to create an arrangement of mixed species, such as daffodils and tulips.

Some bulbs, like paperwhites, hyacinths and crocuses can actually be grown in water, without any soil at all. There are specially shaped vases that can be purchased for forcing bulbs in water, but there are other creative and decorative options as well. A shallow glass bowl filled half way with water and crystal pebbles for the bulbs to rest on is one of many beautiful ideas.

When you see growth beginning, move the pots to a warm, sunny window without allowing plants to touch the glass, and keep them moist. When bulbs are in full bloom they can be relocated to a cooler, more shaded area in the house, like a dining room table or nightstand, to prolong the bloom. It is not necessary to fertilize since bulbs contain all the nutrients they need. For a list of bulb varieties for forcing indoors see Appendix B, p.152.

PLANT LISTS

BULB VARIETIES FOR FORCING INDOORS

Bulbs that do not need chilling

Amaryllis
 'Green Goddess'
 'Salmon Pearl'
 'Scarlet Baby'
 'Star of Holland'
 'Yellow Dancer'
Paperwhites
 'Bethlehem'
 'Galilee'
 'Grand Soleil d'Or'
 'Ziva'

Bulbs that require chilling*

Crocus
 'Jeanne d'Arc'
 'King of the Striped'
 'Pickwick'
 'Purpurea Grandiflora'
 'Remembrance'
 'Victor Hugo'
Daffodil
 'Barrett Browning'
 'Carlton'
 'Dutch Master'
 'Ice Follies'

 'Little Beauty'
 'Little Gem'
 'Texas'
 'Topolino'
Hyacinth
 'Amsterdam'
 'Anna Marie'
 'Bismarck'
 'Carnegie'
 'Jan Bos'
 'L'Innocence'
 'Ostara'
Iris
Muscari
Tulip
 'Attilla'
 'Bestseller'
 'Electra'
 'Hibernia'
 'Inzell'
 'Peach Blossom'
 'Yellow Present'

*Bulbs can usually be purchased prechilled at the nursery or ordered by catalog.

FERNS FOR INDOORS

Adiantum pedatum (maidenhair fern)
Asplenium bulbiferum
Asplenium nidus (bird's nest fern)
Blechnum gibbum (dwarf tree fern)
Dicksonia antarctica (Tasmanian tree fern)
Microlepia strigosa
Nephrolepis exaltata 'Bostoniensis' (Boston fern)
Notholaena spp. (cloak fern)
Onychium japonicum (claw fern)
Pellaea rotundifolia (Button fern)
Platycerium bifurcatum (staghorn fern)
Polypodium aureum (hare's-foot fern)
Pteris cretica 'Albo-lineata' (Variegated table fern)

ORCHIDS FOR INDOORS

Brassolaeliocattleya hybrids
Cattleya hybrids
Cattleya mini orchids
Cymbidium hybrids
Dendrobium Phalaenopsis hybrids
Laeliocattleya hybrids
Miltonia hybrids (pansy orchids)
Odontoglossum hybrids
Oncidium hybrids
Paphiopedilum hybrids (lady's-slipper orchids)
Phalaenopsis equestris hybrids
Phalaenopsis hybrids (moth orchids)
Phragmipedium hybrids
Pleione spp.

PALMS FOR INDOORS

Caryota mitis (Burmese fishtail palm)
C. urens
Chamaedorea elegans (parlor palm)
Chamaedorea erumpens
C. metallica
Cocos Nucifera (coconut palm)
Chrysalidocarpus lutescens (areca palm)
Cyrostachys lakka (lipstick palm)
Euterpe edulis
Hedyscepe canterburyana (umbrella palm)
H. forsterana
Howea belmoreana (sentry palm)
Laccospadix australasica
Phoenix canariensis (Canary date palm)
P. roebelenii (pygmy date palm)
Reinhardtia gracilis
Rhapis excelsa (lady palm)
Washingtonia robusta (thread palm)

PLANTS FOR CHILDREN

Ananas comosus (pineapple)
- The leafy top of an ordinary pineapple can be made to root.

Capsicum annuum (ornamental peppers)
- This is an eye-catching, ornamental plant that will bear fruit.

Dionaea muscipula (Venus's-flytrap)
- This is a fascinating carnivorous plant that eats tiny insects.

Epiphyllum lavi (night-blooming cactus)
- This night-blooming Mexican cactus has exotic, fragrant early summer flowers.

Mimosa pudica (sensitive plant)
- The leaves will fold and droop when touched.

Olea europaea (olive)
- The gray-leafed olive tree can be kept small by pruning in the spring. Older plants produce tiny, fragrant flowers and often bear olives.

Sarracenia flava (yellow pitcher plant)
- This cool-room lover is a carnivorous plant that attracts and consumes insects.

Selaginella lepidophylla (resurrection plant)
- Purchased as a dried, brown ball, the plant will uncurl into a rosette of lush fernlike fronds when placed in a pot of water or damp soil.

Streptocarpus wendlandii (cape primrose)
- This plant is visually unique and interesting with its single, enormous, purple-green basil leaf and blue summer flowers.

PLANTS FOR TERRARIUMS

Adiantum raddianum (delta maidenhair fern)

Bertolonia marmorata

Episcia 'Cleopatra'

E. cupreata (flame violet)

E. lilacina

Ficus pumila 'White Sonny' (creeping fig)

Fittonia verschaffeltii (mosaic plant)

Hypoestes phyllostachya (baby's tears)

H. phyllostachya 'Vinrod'

Maranta leuconeura var. *erythroneura* (red herringbone plant)

Peperomia caperata 'Little Fantasy'

P. obtusifolia

Pilea cadierei (aluminum plant)

Pilea involucrata 'Norfolk' (friendship plant)

P. involucrate 'Moon Valley'

Saintpaulia 'Blue Imp' (African violet)

S. 'Pip Squeak'

Selaginella uncinata (peacock moss)

S. kraussiana 'Aurea' (golden dwarf club moss)

PLANTS THAT CLEAN THE AIR

Araucaria heterophylla (Norfolk Island pine)

Begonia semperflorens (wax begonia)

Brassaia actinophylla (schefflera, Australian umbrella tree)

Chamaedorea elegans (parlor palm)

C. seifrizii (bamboo palm)

Chrysalidocarpus lutescens (areca palm)

Chrysanthemum morifolium (mum)

Dieffenbachia 'Exotica Compacta' (dumb cane)

Dracaena deremensis 'Janet Craig'

D. deremensis 'Warneckei'

D. fragrans 'Massangeana' (corn plant)

D. marginata (dragon tree)

Epipremnum aureum (golden pothos)

F. elastica (rubber plant)

Gerbera jamesonii (gerbera daisy)

Hedera helix (English ivy)

Nephrolepis exaltata 'Bostoniensis' (Boston fern)

Philodendron erubescens (red-leaf philodendron)

P. oxycardium (heart-leaf philodendron)

P. selloum (lacy tree philodendron)

Phoenix roebelenii (pygmy date palm)

Rhapis excelsa (lady palm)

Sansevieria trifasciata (snake plant)

Spathiphyllum sp. (peach lily)

Syngonium podophyllum (arrowhead vine)

PLANTS FOR BEGINNING HYDROCULTURE

Low light

Aglaonema modestum (Chinese evergreen)

Dracaena deremensis 'Janet Craig'

Ficus lyrata (fiddle-leaf fig)

Hedera helix (ivy)

Philodendron

Schefflera (umbrella tree)

Spathiphyllum (peace lily)

Medium light

Anthurium

Dieffenbachia (dumb cane)

Ficus benjamina (weeping fig)

Ficus elastica (rubber plant)

Hoya spp. (wax vine)

Pandanus spp. (screw pine)

Peperomia spp.

Sansevieria trifasciata (snake plant)

Vriesea splendens (flaming sword)

High light

Araucaria heterophylla (Norfolk Island pine)

Cacti (all varieties)

Codiaeum variegatum (croton)

Dracaena marginata (dragon tree)

Succulents (most varieties)

SUCCULENTS FOR INDOORS

Aeonium 'Zwartkop' (black aeonium)

Borzicactus trollii (old man of the Andes)

Crassula falcate (airplane plant)

Echinocactus grusonii (barrel cactus)

Echinocereus pectinatus (rainbow cactus)

Euphorbia obesa (living baseball)

Gymnocalycium mihanovichii 'Red Cap' (plain cactus)

Lithops salicola (living stone)

Mammillaria hahniana (old lady cactus)

M. zeilmanniana 'Ubinkii' (rose pincushion)

Opuntia microdasys (rabbit-ears)

O. verschaffeltii

Pachyphytum oviferum (moonstones)

Rebutia spegazziniana

Rhipsalis cereuscula (coral cactus)

Schlumbergera truncata (crab cactus)

Sedum morganianum (donkey's tail)

S. pachyphyllum (many-fingers)

Selenicereus grandiflorus (queen-of-the-night)

GARDEN DESIGNERS, CONSULTANTS, AND LANDSCAPE ARCHITECTS

The Green Man
Scott D. Appell
83 Wooster Street
New York, NY 10012-4376
(212) 966-4745
(212) 966-0527 (fax)

Living Green Plantscape
Davis Dalbok
3 Henry Adams
San Francisco, CA 94103
(415) 864-2251
(415) 864-6355 (fax)
livgrn@pacbell.net

Craig Bergmann Landscape Design, Inc.
1924 Lake Avenue
Wilmette, IL 60091
(847) 251-8355

P. Clifford Miller, Inc
11 N. Skokie Blvd. #200
Lake Bluff, IL 60044
(874) 234-6664

Deborah Nevins and Associates
270 Lafayette Street #903
New York, NY 10012
(212) 925-1125

Rob Girard, Horticultural Consultant
8 Thomas Lane
New Milford, CT 06776
(860) 210-1373

Edwina von Gal & Company
42-24 Ninth Street,
Long Island City, NY 11101
(718) 706-6007
(718) 937-1725 (fax)

Morgan Wheelock Incorporated
Landscape Architectural Design
444 Bunker Road, Suite 201
West Palm Beach, FL 33405
(561) 585-8577
www.morganwheelock.com

ARCHITECTS

McAlpine Tankersley Architecture, Inc.
644 South Perry Street
Montgomery, AL 36104
(334) 262-8315
(334) 269-1637 (fax)
www.mcalpinetankersley.com

Warren Platner Associates Architects
18 Mitchell Drive
New Haven, CT 06511
(203) 777-6471

Leta Austin Foster and Associates, Inc
64 Via Mizner
Palm Beach, FL 33480
(561) 655-5489
(561) 655-3027 (fax)

Hammond Beeby Rupert Ainge Architects
440 N. Wells Street #630
Chicage, IL 60610
(312) 527-3200

SKA Architect + Planner
Jacqueline Albarran AIA
204 Phipps Plaza
Palm Beach, FL 33480
(561) 655-7676
(561) 655-3533 (fax)
jadmska@earthlink.net

Robert Stewart Burton Architects
65 Pondfield Road
Bronxfield, NY 10708
(914) 779-2171

INTERIOR DESIGNERS

McAlpine Booth & Ferrier Interiors, Inc.
Cummins Station Suite 223
209 10th Avenue South
Nashville, TN 37203
(615) 259-1222
(615) 259-1250 (fax)
www.mcalpineboothferrier.com

Embellishments for the Home
Elizabeth Love DePedro
4131 Burns Road
Palm Beach Gardens, FL 33410
(561) 691-9281

Brown Davis Interiors
2 Via Las Incas
Palm Beach, FL 33480
(561) 514-3034

ARTIST

Yaz Krehbiel Paintings
930 Rosemary Road
Lake Forest, IL 60045
(847) 234-6362

URBAN GARDENS/ROOF TERRACE DESIGNERS

Halsted Welles Associates
287 East Houston Street
New York, NY 10002
(212) 777-5440
(212) 777-2043 (fax)
hwa@halstedwelles.com

CONSERVATORY COMPANIES

Amdega Conservatories
16 Ostend Avenue
Westport, CT 06880
(800) 761-9183
www.amdega.com

Marston and Langinger Limited
192 Ebury Street
London
SWIW 8UP
North American Sales
www.marston-and-langinger.com

RARE PLANTS

Another Place in Time
1101 Tulane Street
Houston, TX 77008
(713) 864-9717
www.anotherplaceintime.com
mlowery5@aol.com

PONDS

Pond Works
Rex Wilroy, Owner
P.O. Box 820368
Houston, TX 77282-0368
(281) 693-4742
(281) 773-5519 (fax)
kirby2@mail.ev1.net

WATER GARDENS

Nelson Water Gardens and Nursery
1502 Katy Fort Bend County Road
Katy, Texas 77493
(281) 391-4769
www.nelsonwatergardens.com

NONPROFIT ORGANIZATIONS

Drylands Institute
Richard Felger, Ph.D.,
Executive Director
PMB 405, 2509 North Campbell
Avenue
Tucson, AZ 85719

American Orchid Society
16700 AOS Lane
Delray Beach, FL 33446-4351
(561) 404-2000
(561) 404-2100 (fax)
TheAOS@aos.org

The American Daffodil Society, Inc.
4126 Winfield Road
Columbus, OH 43220-4606
(614) 451-4747
(614) 451-2177 (fax)
www.daffodilusa.org

American Begonia Society
Arlene Ingles
157 Monument
Rio Dell, CA 95562-1617
(707) 764-5407
www.begonias.org

Indoor Gardening Society of America
Sharon Zentz-President
944 South Munroe Road
Tallmadge, OH 44278
(216) 733-8414
www.indoorgarden.org

American Horticultural Society
7931 East Boulevard Drive
Alexandria, VA 22308
(703) 768-5700
(703) 768-8700 (fax)
www.ahs.org

Acknowledgments

My thanks go to the many gardeners all over the United States who, after receiving an inquiring call from a complete stranger, graciously welcomed me into their homes, served me at their tables, and guided me into their glorious indoor gardens. Their warm hospitality, good humor, and gardening genius helped make writing this book a treasured experience.

I send a warm thanks to the many professionals who offered their guidance and expertise. Paul Zec and Miranda Kettlewell gave me hours of their time, drove me all over the countryside, and directed me to some of the most beautiful sites. Marya Padour was a kind and gracious garden guide who helped to ease the burden of a grueling travel schedule. Wayne Boddie and Brian Krapff from Amdega Conservatories, Darren Duling from the American Orchid Society, David Eppele, Anita Nelson from Nelson's Watergardens in Houston, and Bob Fuchs from RF Orchids in Florida were some of the many professionals who were so patient and generous with their time. Friends like Barbara Harrison, Ann Cunningham, and Tom and Kathy Leahy guided me to gardens that have enriched this book. Shirley Milligan, Ken Johnson, Don Larsen, Roland Rooso, Alexandra Taylor, members of the Hollerith family, and Hilary Wonham helped find files, supply old photographs, answer questions, schedule appointments, and fill in the many gaps that helped to assure accurateness in these pages.

Marisa Bulzone from Stewart Tabori & Chang is a friend as well as a perceptive and creative editor, and her expertise and faith in this project helped it to be born. She and her team, designer Nina Barnett; assistant editor Elaine Schiebel, and Kim Tyner in production, helped to make this book beautiful.

John Hall's stunning photography made my vision of this book a reality. Alan Nevins is a wise and helpful representative, and I am immensely grateful for his help.

To all my friends, whose invitations I continually declined in favor of long hours with the keyboard, a special gratitude for not giving up on me.

This book is dedicated to my loving husband Joe, for being my biggest fan, and for his consistent encouragement and very good humor even as I traded his companionship for my Gateway 2000 computer.

Thanks to Michela, who listened eagerly, whose creativity and perception continually generated new ideas, and whose pride in my work was always a huge source of encouragement; to Angelina, whose determination for me, loving efforts, and endless hours of toil on my behalf, with babe on hip, made it possible for me to complete this book; to Joseph, who inspires with his poetry, was always there to laugh with me, revive my on-line connection, and commiserate as he labored for the bar exam; to Alexander, whose love of the arts and the written word, pride for my work, and encouragement was always an inspiration; to my beautiful new daughter Margaret, who cared for me when I was in New York; to Danny and Tom, both talented writers, who by giving us our two newest family members, Magdalena and Nicholas, fill us with endless joy; to my sister, Julie Driscoll Farrah, for her constant support of my work, for reading the draft of this book, and for her sensitive and insightful commentary in the margins, which were always right on target. And to another multi-talented sister Theresa Driscoll Moore, a true Renaissance woman, attorney and photographer, who produced my portrait for this book.

A final thanks to Stella and Stanley, who were there to keep me company and always kept my feet warm.